Tik

with

TikTok SEO & Algorithm

Ultimate Money Guide

#TikTok Influencer #TikTok Entrepreneur

#TikTok Success #TikTok Monetization

#Social Media Influencer Marketing

@ InvestingWizard Press

Copyright © 2021 by Investing Wizard

Legal Disclaimer:

Please note that the information in this book is for educational and informational purposes only. The purpose of this book is to provide information with currently available knowledge and understanding based on the author's best efforts at that time without any kind, express, or implied warranty. It is NOT intended to be used as a substitute for any advice (including but not limited to) Legal, Technology, investing, and Medical, or any other services.

Readers should use their judgment and own advisors for all decisions and should not base or rely on this book for any decisions. We disclaim all warranties or implied warranties concerning all content on this book. Readers should consult their business professionals or licensed professional for any business and investing advice. Readers should consult an attorney for any legal advice.

The author(s) have made every effort to provide accurate, reliable, and up-to-date information, while due to the possibility of human errors or change/updates, author(s) do not guarantee that all information included is complete or accurate, and disclaim all responsibilities for any omissions or error, or the results obtained from using the information contained in this document.

Author(s) has no obligation to warrant the accuracy or appropriateness of any third-party websites or URLs. The listing of any person, business, hyperlinks, or others in this book does not constitute an endorsement or recommendation by the author(s). If a reader chooses to click on links and be taken to an external website belonging to a third party, then the reader and only the reader shall be responsible and liable for his/her actions should you suffer or incur any harm or loss from the usage of such information.

By reading this, the reader agrees that under no circumstances is the author(s) responsible for any direct or indirect losses incurred due to using this document's information, including not limited to omissions, inaccuracies, or errors. You agree to hold the author(s) harmless from ALL (including but not limited to) claims, losses, damages, etc.

Table of Contents

Introduction

Do you want to attract loyal followers and create a highly successful personal brand?

Are you thinking about becoming the next TikTok star to make money from this hot social media platform?

Are you a business owner or a brand manager looking for more traffic to expand your market via TikTok?

If your answer is **YES** to any of the above questions, then keep reading.

It seems that a new social-media platform redefines the way people interact online almost every decade. We can also see videos go viral every day, but recently, a large chunk of them came straight from a single source: TikTok. Yes, TikTok is taking over. Even though not everyone likes it, but no one can deny its popularity.

Not being on TikTok seems to be a HUGE mistake. This platform provides a unique way to make and spread ideas and has become one of the biggest social networks worldwide. There are already 2 billion users who have downloaded TikTok, and it is available in over 200 countries, which means TikTok is a fertile ground for organic reach and paid advertising. It's not uncommon for a TikToker to earn $4000-$5000 per post. Many TikTok influencers are able to make even much more. For example, the college student Addison Rae can make about $15,000 per sponsored post. This is the platform that can help you earn six figures easier than you thought.

If you think TikTok is just for Gen Z, think again. When you explore TikTok, you'll find various brands advertising on it in industries like clothing, eCommerce, streaming, beauty, mobile apps, and many more. You can definitely use this platform to your business's advantage.

Most people think that they can just jump on it and easily get their piece. However, once they try, it seems like they don't have that magic power. No strategy equals a significant loss. TikTok is no exception to this rule. This is why it's super risky to start without a comprehensive guide to TikTok marketing.

Also, every social media platform has its own unwritten rule. You can break your business if you just ignore them. So how can you succeed on TikTok exactly? How can you attract millions of followers and convert those followers to dollars? How can you make your content go viral and monetize from it?

That's why our insiders create this *TikTok Marketing with TikTok SEO & Algorithm* with actionable advice and strategic planning to help you kickstart a profitable TikTok business as well as expand your TikTok empire. This book provides all the answers and is your ONE STOP SHOP for all your TikTok needs.

Inside, you will learn:

- Understand TikTok Better To **Level Up** Your TikTok Game;
- How To Find Your Own **Profitable TikTok Niche**;
- How To **Optimize** Your TikTok Profile;
- How To Use TikTok **Algorithm** And Metrics To Succeed On TikTok;
- How To Use **TikTok SEO** To Make Your Content **Go Viral** And Get **More Engagement And Followers;**
- How To Master **Influencer Marketing;**
- How To **Monetize** Your TikTok Account For The Maximum Profits;
- Best **TikTok Tools** To Triple Your TikTok Account;
- How To **Safely Protect** Your TikTok Account

... much more.

This is Not a theoretical presentation. This straight-to-the-point book is full of updated knowledge and proven strategies, aiming to help you earn, grow, and automate making money of TikTok. You will get the right roadmap to rapidly grow your TikTok accounts, build your personal brand, expand your business, and make fruitful marketing efforts.

Even if you have already got an online presence on

Youtube, Instagram, or Facebook, being active on TikTok will help you gain an even wider audience. This guide discloses all you need to know about TikTok. Whether you are a (future) social media influencer, business owner, or brand manager, _**TikTok Marketing with TikTok SEO & Algorithm**_ is your ticket to building real influence as well as an enjoyable, profitable, and deeply rewarding business.

Don't leave this opportunity on the table. Master the world of TikTok and grow your TikTok business like a pro!

Bonus:

Thank you for purchasing this book!

You can get an _**TikTok Hashtag Playbook**_ & updates on this book for FREE by scanning the above QR code.

Section: Understand TikTok Better to Level Up Your TikTok Game

1 . TikTok – The Fastest Growing New Social Media

TikTok, known as "Douyin" in China, was launched in September 2016. At that time, Facebook already had more than 1.5 billion users, and Instagram has over 600 million. No one could have guessed that TikTok could become so popular.

In 2017, TikTok became available on Google Play and the Apple store for all users worldwide. The dizzying growth of users started in 2018.

Until now, TikTok is one of the fastest-growing social media platforms enabling users to share short videos ranging from 15 seconds to 3 minutes long. It has the most downloads globally. While Instagram and Facebook record annual member growth of around 5 to 10%, TikTok's growth is over 30% for the second year in a row. After TikTok merged with Musical.ly, it becomes a mix between Vine and Musicl.ly. People began to use it even more.

TikTok users are filming videos that are getting millions of views, and many TikTok influencers have millions of followers. The top ten most followed Tiktok accounts have more than 20 million followers, and social media personalities own most of them. We can also see that more and more stars are gaining popularity just based on TikTok content.

Although practically speaking, it's not possible for TikTok to dethrone Facebook, it has certainly secured its place among the top five social medial platforms. (The other top four are Facebook, Youtube, Instagram, What's App.)

2. Why is TikTok So Popular?

Now, you may wonder why TikTok is so popular. Besides people are more accepting of social medial platforms and the smartphone make the technology behind it possible, there are a few more reasons that make TikTok so popular:

- **The appeal of TikTok content**

It's true that many platforms allow people to make short videos, while what's special about TikTok? The **video length** is probably the most important reason of all. The 15s-3m long videos can give its users much freedom as they may need.

TikTok's another benefit is that you are allowed to make any type of video with any songs you love, such as dancing, tricks, lip-syncing, pranks. You can also do it alone or with friends.

Its **remix feature** is especially appealing. People are able to take other users' videos and add them to their own videos, either make a joke or mimic their movements. And this can go on for quite a while. Users can keep this trendy chain going until the videos become hard to understand or gets too confusing.

Their recently implemented advertising system is not yet as annoying as Facebook and Instagram, which can be another reason it's popular. Social media platforms can easily drive users away by starting pelting users with ads.

We can imagine it will attract another a few more million users easily if they can come up with new stuff.

- **TikTok Challenges**

Still remember when people were all about those weird Youtube challenges a few years back? When they would film themselves stuffing their mouths with cinnamon and really hot peppers? This time is not over yet. Challenges are still happening on YouTube as well as TikTok.

Jimmy Fallon started #Thumbleweedchallenge in 2018, where people record themselves rolling on the ground like the tumbleweeds with the western music playing in the background. This challenge not only brought him a ton of publicity but also started a new popular TikTok trend making people more than eager to join.

If we imagine a brand starting this kind of popular challenge, it would improve its brand image and boost sales. Even if the brand is not that famous with a small following, they still can hire popular influencers to start a challenge for them.

- **TikTok "For You" Page (FYP)**

FYP is a content discovery feed powered by AI and certainly worth a big credit for TikTok's success. Its unique algorithm will show users the best content based on your browsing history and your interest. The AI behind it pays attention to what content you watched, liked, commented on, as well as what content you posted.

Besides above, the algorithm also analyzes the interests of those whose videos you watch, which is very similar to choices like "frequently bought together."

This high-level algorithm is still being improved constantly, so we should attribute it to these developers who have done a great job and attracted millions of users.

Yes, other social media networks have something similar to the FYP, but none is as successful as TikTok's.

- **More and more celebrities**

It's noticeable that more and more celebrities are joining TikTok too. On Tiktok, you will find Jason Derulo, Selena Gomez, Will Smith, Justin Beiber, Mariah Carey, Alex Rodrigues, and many more.

Many of those who haven't created a TikTok

account will make one as their favorite celebrity is on it.

- **More and more people of different age groups**

What has happened to Facebook is now happening to TikTok. History always repeats itself. Now, more and more people of different age groups are joining TikTok, either for fun or to promote their business. We are seeing more 30s, 40s, and above are actively on TikTok, which undoubtedly contributes to TikTok being so popular.

- **Facebook isn't cool anymore**

Statistics show that 94% of teens were using Facebook in 2012, but that number is now down to less than 50%. Nothing lasts forever, and the popularity of social media platforms is no exception.

Nowadays, teens just don't think Facebook is cool anymore. TikTok is the new hot trend. It's easier for anyone to film something and get hundreds of views even if they don't have lots of followers.

Another thing that might contribute to teens leaving Facebook for TikTok is the fact that more and more parents, even grandparents, are using Facebook. Teens may not try to hide something, but they still don't want them to embarrass themselves and pray for their parents not to show interest in Facebook.

3. Who Are the Main TikTok Users

We can notice that TikTok is strongly youth-oriented. As the parent generation is spending time on their Facebook accounts, Generation Z wants their own social spaces. Based on the data from June 2021, the largest group on TikTok are aged between 16 and 24 (30-39: 16.4%, 40-49: 13.9%, 50+: 7.1%). These users make up 41% of the total. While as mentioned, since TikTok provides a fantastic opportunity to promote business, there are more and more older generations are joining.

When it comes to gender, 47% of TikTok users are female, and 53% are male. In the U.S market specifically, 60% are female, and 40% are male.

4. What Types of Content Do Well

Similar to YouTube, the heart of TikTok is the videos that people like to share. Typically, the more entertaining the videos, the better they can resonate with the audience. But unlike Youtube, the videos are short and filmed in a vertical format.

Home-made music videos are still performing well on TikTok. The original music is even more popular than cover versions. However, they offer fewer opportunities for delivering promotional messages compared to other kinds of video.

Surely, there's now more non-music video on TikTok. Many of them are comedic. Others include cringe videos, cooking demonstrations, fashion and beauty tips, short skits, and even sports action short clips.

One absolute worst mistake is to post anything resembling the traditional advertisement on TikTok. Instead, even if you want to advertise your products, make it like storytelling and keep it authentic.

5. Drive Engagement: TikTok Most Notable Features & Hidden Features

Whether you want to become a TikTok influencer or you are one of the most TikTok influencers, knowing the TikTok features is going to do a lot to make your content even better. It's advisable to play around with the app – the more you use it, the better your content will be.

5.1 TikTok Most Notable Features

- **Video editing tools**

Similar to Snapchat, TikTok enables users to edit the videos with an impressive toolset of video effects, including adding stickers, animations, masks, slow-motion effects, changing the color of the eyes, and many more.

- **Reactions**

TikTokers can create videos with their response to others' music videos and publish them in their own feed. To do this, tap the **share** button on the right side of the screen, and choose **React.** Now you can tap the record button and add your effects.

Pro tip: Some creators will script their reactions, and it's more fun to only record a genuine reaction.

- **Sounds**

Users can add favorite songs as background music to their videos from the built-in TikTok library. The lip-syncing feature is popular here.

- **Geolocation**

TikTok can display active bloggers nearby and how are broadcasting streams.

- **Social sharing**

You can share your videos edited on TikTok on your Facebook, Instagram, and YouTube profiles.

- **Live streaming**

With this premium TikTok feature, creators can use live streams to receive goods from their fans bought with TikTok coins.

- **Duet option**

The duets are the videos with a split screen where the original one is on the right and the new video from the user who created the duet on the left. TikTokers can make music videos with lip sync and add the hashtag of **#duewithme**, inviting other TikTokers to duet with them.

If you want to duet with others' video, just find the video you desire to duet with, and then click the "**share**" button on the right. Next, tap Duet, record your own clip by tapping the **record** button and edit it as you want.

- **QR code scanner**

People can scan a unique QR code to subscribe to their favorite accounts.

5.2 TikTok Hidden Feature with Hacks

After knowing TikTok's notable features, would you believe there are even more to it? Now, we're going to cover a whopping 16 hidden features with hacks to take your TikTok content to new heights as well as make your life much easier as a content creator.

Are you excited? Let's get started!

1. **Choose when the text appears and disappears**

Many times, we just want to add text only at certain points in the videos. Luckily, Tiktok makes it easy to do so.

After you create a video, click "**Aa Text**" at the bottom. After finishing typing your text, click "**Done**."

To set the duration, tap your text box again and choose **"Set duration."** From there, you will see a new small screen with all the frames from your video at the bottom. Now, you can drag and drop the starting and ending of the red bar to where you prefer the text to show up and stop. If you are happy with how it's set up, press the checkmark to finish.

Your text then will only appear during the point in your video that you set it to show up. You can take advantage of this feature to create a truly fantastic video.

2. Create your own slideshow

You can use the templated provided by TikTok to create a slideshow, while wouldn't you rather make a custom one stand out? Here's a simple hack you can use to make a customed slideshow.

After you filming your intro as you normally do, go to **Effects** and select **Green Screen**.

The next step is to choose an image you want to use from your camera roll as the background and tilt your phone so that you won't be visible on the screen, which can allow your picture to fill the entire screen. At the same time, you can film and release along with audio or music.

To build a slideshow, repeat this process and film for another few seconds. When you are done, you will get a custom one that's exactly what you want it to be without limiting yourself to these templates.

3. Adjust TikTok clips

Sometimes you filmed longer than you wanted, or you just want to change the order or length of your clips after you filmed your video. Tap the **Adjust Clips** button to do this.

After you enter the Adjust Clips screen, you can drag and drop clips to change their order or tap on the clip you want to change the length.

This feature is perfect for complicated transitions where you want to get the timing just right.

4. Record a Voiceover or Vlog

Many TikTokers love to record a voiceover or vlog for their daily lives. To do this, you can film your TikTok videos as you usually do, then click **Next** to go to the posting screen. It is where you usually type in your hashtags and captions. Rather than posting your TikTok, you will begin recording your screen (ensure that your microphone is on.)

Pro tip: For better effects, turn the volume on your phone all the way down to avoid hearing the audio from the TikTok recording when you are recording the audio of your voiceover.

After you finish, you can watch the preview of your video by tapping on your video's thumbnail to the right of the caption.

Then when you are watching the video, narrate what's happening in this video clip. Both what you are saying and what's happening on your screen will be recorded by your phone. After you finish, close the TikTok preview and stop the screen recording.

The next step is opening screen recording from your camera roll, trim the beginning and end of it as you like. You want to leave only the actual contents without showing you starting and stopping the screen recording.

Now, it's time to go into TikTok and tap on the **Upload** icon. Select the screen recording video from your camera roll and post as the way you usually do.

5. Save without the TikTok logo

Sometimes, you will want to post your TikTok videos to other platforms but don't want it to look like a repurposed content. In those cases, you want to get that TikTok logo out of your video.

To achieve this, start screen recording with your microphone off and volume tuned up before you post your TikTok.

Also, watch the preview of the screen recording several times to make sure that you get all you want from your video. Then, close the preview and end the screen recording.

Open that screen recording from your camera roll and trim it to capture the wanted parts of that video.

Now you get the desired video that looks like native content without logos. You can use it on Facebook, Instagram, Youtube, or whichever other social media platforms you use.

6. Use songs from others

Just stumble across a TikTok with a sound you want to use? It's easy to add songs and sounds from other creators' TikToks to your videos. Also, you can do it without making a duet with the person.

If you like the background sound, just tap that music track at the bottom, and then you will see all the videos using this sound on the next screen.

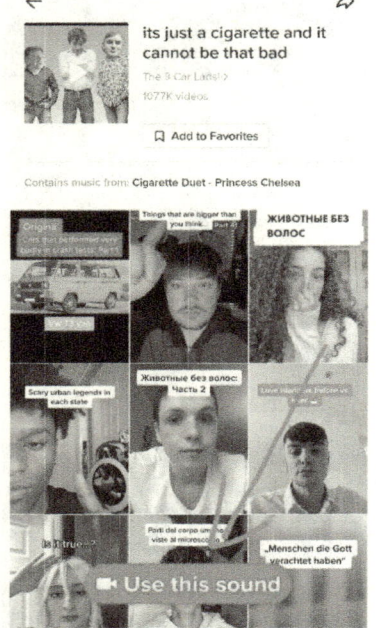

To use the sound, tap **"Use this sound"** at the bottom center of the screen, which will take you to the recording screen. When you begin recording your video, this sound will play so that you will be able to make a lip-syn video or do whatever you want with this sound.

7. Create custom TikTok Audio

Besides using audio from other users, you can also create your own. Of course, you can use a single audio song or file, while we are going to kick it up a notch in this example: merging two different trendy sounds to make new audio.

The first step is finding videos using the songs you want to use, then tap the **Share** button to bring up sharing choices. Then, click "**Save Video**" to save it to your camera roll.

After you save both videos, now it's time to open up your favorite mobile video editing app, import the TikTok videos you just downloaded for the audio.

You can begin to split, trim, and move clips around to make a new audio file as you want. You don't need to worry about the video part since nobody will see it.

Save it to your camera roll once you are happy with your sound. Then head back to TikTok, upload the video you just made.

Remember to change the **privacy settings** from **Public** to **Private** before posting the video so that others won't see this not-ready version.

After you post your private video, go to your profile and tap on the video. Then find the **spinning record** icon in the screen's lower right corner, and choose "**Use this sound**."

Now you can use your freshly-made custom audio to make your TikTok video.

8. Name your audio for search

After you put your efforts into creating a custom sound that you are proud of, you probably will want to make sure other TikTokers can find it and use it too. To make this happen, open a video where you used your audio. In the lower right corner of the screen, find and tap on the spinning record icon.

Then click the **Edit** button next to the title and change to whatever you like. Tap **Save** once you are happy with it.

Please note that TikTok will only let you change your audio's title once, so make sure to get it right the first time.

9. Make a GIF

You may miss you if you haven't started using GIF marketing. GIFs are popular because they are short while engaging with an emotional punch.

To make a shareable GIF from TikTok, find a video you want to convert and click the **share** button. Then, tap **Share as GIF.** Now you can save it directly to your phone or share it.

While please note that GIFs created from TikTok will be watermarked.

10. Translate a comment

As you get more and more attention on your video and even become a TikTok influencer, you are likely to get a comment in another language that you don't understand. No worries. TikTok provides a translation tool that will help you translate those comments easily.

To translate the comment in a foreign language, just tap and hold the comment to bring up a menu.

From there, choose **Translate**. Then TikTok will translate the comment into the language you set up in your profile.

6. What's New For TikTok

1. TikTok Tipping Via Coins & Icons

TikTokers can use Text2Shop, a MagicLinks exclusive influencer monetization technology, enabling your fans to shop your social content just by a single text message.

The TikTok Coins and Icons can be purchased for as little as $0.99 for 100 coins (while the cost and amount can change with currency market swings and inflation.) Then these coins can be gifted to creators, who will be able to redeem them for cash, which is similar to YouTube LiveStream Super Chats. It may not make lots of money in a short time, but you should still add a call to action: "donate some coins to me" in your captions.

You can turn the coins you received into TikTok Diamonds after receiving enough icons and coins and then changing them into cash through PayPal. While at this time, only TikTok accounts with >1,000 followers are able to accept coin and icon gifts.

2. Live stream Shopping

TikTok live stream shopping is a new eCommerce experience allowing users to buy items from participating online retailers in live-streaming events.

When TikTok videos are playing, the products are shown on-screen, and the pop-up pins will also appear related to items on the video. Then the viewers can tap on these pins to add what they like to their cart, which will direct them to a mobile checkout page. Also, the viewers can also choose to wait until the event is finished and click on their shopping cart pins to check all the items featured in the event and chose which ones they decide to buy.

3. New TikTok caption features

Everyone deserves to be capable of participating in social media. TikTok has already launched many features to help accessibility:

- Text-to-speech for users with visual impairments;
- The option to replace those animated video thumbnails with static images.
- Creator warnings that will notify creators before they upload video with photosensitive content that may trigger epilepsy;
- Photosensitivity filters to enable users with migraines or epilepsy can skip those photosensitive content;

Auto-generated TikTok captions are being rolled out. At present, this feature only includes American English and Japanese, and other languages will be added over time. After you've recorded or uploaded a video, choose auto-captions on the editing page. If desired, you can also edit caption text after it's generated. Additionally, TikTok is working with accessibility nonprofits, such as the Deaf Collective, to increase its usability for all.

4. TikTok playlists

Playlists and highlights reels can help fans discover more of the types of your content they want to watch. Organizing your TikTok content into playlists is a vital component of your brand. Consider using playlists to create themed collections, including long-form series or tutorials.

To create TikTok creator playlists, go to your profile, and tap **Sort videos into Playlists.** Then name your **playlist**, choose the videos you want to include, then tap **Save**. You'll find your playlist in your bio.

Please note that only public videos can be added to TikTok Playlists, and videos can only appear on one Playlist at a time.

5. TikTok Music Visualizer

Recently, TikTok has launched new VR music effects. The music visualizer is the first-ever music creative effect on Tiktok. Now, TikTokers now can create animations instantly. It's a set of interactive tools shown on screen when you record. Use it to your advantage to custom-craft videos that can stand out.

6. Jumps feature

TikTok just announced another amazing feature called "Jumps," allowing creators to link third-party-owned mini-programs or services from their video clips, such as quizzes, recipes, and more.

When users are watching a video with a Jump, they will see a button near the bottom of the screen, which will open another small new screen within TikTok. Creators can customize the content that users can see after they tap on the Jump.

Section: Find Your Own Profitable TikTok Niche

As the number of TikTok accounts is growing fast, it gets more competitive on the platform. Jumping on TikTok challenges and trends is one way to build your followers and audience. While the other way is to carve out a niche and perfect your content not only to attract a more engaged audience but also to make yourself a name on TikTok.

Users love discovering creators who have their own specialism. If your niche appeals to them, they know they will always find quality content that can interest them from your profile. No matter it's home styling, cooking, comedy skits, or fashion tips, your niche is going to attract like-minded people who will be more likely to engage with your content.

This will also help grow your audience in the long run. When users scroll through their For You page and find your video suited to a specific category they love, they will probably click on your profile and find a collection of similar ones. To receive more of this great content in their Following feed, they will choose to follow you. Your followers will grow steadily over time.

1. What Is A TikTok Niche

A TikTok niche is a smaller subsection of the huge market. For instance, TikToker bomanizer focuses on creating hilarious reality TV shows and has gained millions of views.

When you narrow down a market, you can find areas with much fewer competitors. Even though your audience will be smaller, they will be more likely to engage with your content and share. Just similar to other social media platforms, the most important factor in making money on TikTok is having an engaged audience. And the niche audience will work the best for this.

Some incredibly entertaining and talented TikTok creators have found their niche and keep delivering high-quality content. The following are several more creator examples to inspire you:

- **Parkerlocke** is a very talented editor who films his front yard and turns into TV shows like the Walking Dead and the movie worlds like Harry Potter.

- **Twin.nwin** shares light-hearted and soothing videos of making her favorite recipes to life.

- **Drcody_dc** promotes his chiropractic clinic on TikTok, where he shares small clips from sessions with clients to show his work.

2. How to Find Profitable A TikTok Niche

The simple answer is to do niche research. The following tasks will help you to find the best TikTok niches.

1. **Niche market analysis**. This can help you find potential rising market opportunities. You want to make sure that the market you are planning to target is using this platform.

2. **Niche trends research**. Trens can tell you what people are interested in.

3. **Study competitors in the niche**. You will have a better idea of whether the target niche will work or not. Some niches have many big competitors, and it's better to avoid those.

4. **Find the right audience**. At the time of writing, the major audience on TikTok is generation Z, which makes up 60% of the total users.

Now let's dive into each step.

3. How to Find A Profitable Niche Market

A niche market is one of the sections of the large market and can be defined by its own requirements and needs, targeting a particular group of people. On the other hand, large markets target a wider audience with broader interests.

Simply put, you need to find a specific problem that affects a specific group of audience and then provide the ideal solutions for them. It's a process to find potential customers as well as smaller competition and create a niche product for your ideal customers.

However, it's super important to do deep-dive research on whether the niche can be profitable or not. For example, If you discover a market with little even no competition, it's probably that this is not a profitable niche market. In comparison, if you can find at least some competitors, it may be a sign that this niche market can be potentially profitable.

Pro tip: To capitalize on a niche market, the trick is finding a segment where other people are already spending money, doesn't have aggressive competition, and there's room for continuing growth.

The trick to capitalizing on a niche market is finding a segment where people are already spending money, there is room for growth, and there is no aggressive competition.

Here are several methods you can use to find a niche market idea:

Method #1: Google Suggestions

Step 1: Go to Google, begin typing in its search bar the terms that you are interested in, and Google will suggest some ideas according to what other people are searching:

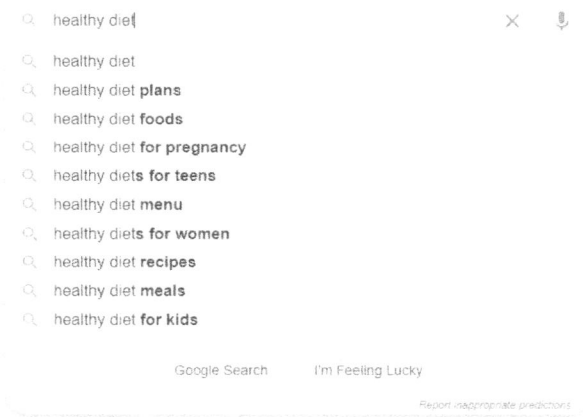

Step 2: Keep niching them down by simply adding words to the right or left of your keyword to get more Google suggestions.

This is a very fast and effective trick to find niche market ideas.

Method #2: Wikipedia

Step 1: Like method #1, go to Wikipedia, type your niche keyword in the search bar, and click on the desired search result.

Step 2: Skim the next page for the sub-niches ideas. The following is an example of the "Diet" niche. In the table of contents, you can see many niche market ideas:

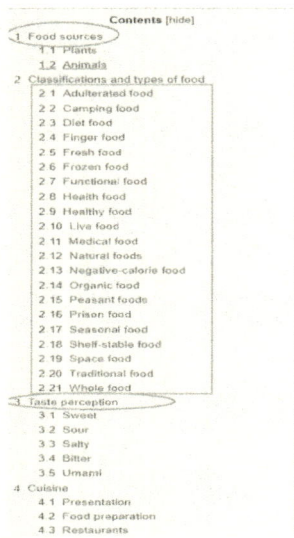

If you want more niche ideas, just click on the terms you are interested in. This is a great way to brainstorm niche ideas.

Method #3 <u>Anser the Public</u>

This approach cannot be more efficient and straightforward.

Step 1: Go to <u>Anser the Public</u>. Type what you are interested in and click **Search**.

Step 2: You will find many niche ideas. This free website does the brainstorming for you, and you can simply choose what attracts you the most. Sweet and straight to the point.

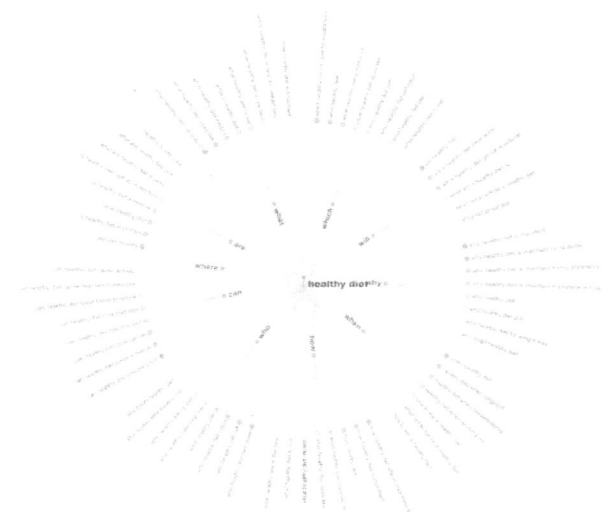

4. How To Validate Your Niche Market Idea (Niche Trends & More)

Now you have a list with some potential ideas. It's time to validate them and choose the best.

The first step will be to confirm if there will be enough audience for your selected niche to make it profitable. If your niche's audience is too small, you may struggle to generate enough traffic and income.

Here are several ways to validate your niche market ideas:

Method #1 Niche trends

To check whether your niche idea is profitable, we need to check if it has an interest. There are some approaches you can use.

1. **Google Trends**

Simply head to Google Trends. Type your niche idea in the search bar. After you get the search result, you can filter by location (whether worldwide or your targeted location) and time frame, which can give you a better idea of how the trend varies by location and over time.

Pro tip: Filter the research results by "Youtube search" because TikTok users are usually more aligned to Youtube Search compared to website search.

Then analyze the trend. Is it stable or growing over time? You want to stay away from trends that have been dropped dramatically over time or with very little interest.

2. **Exploding Topics**

This is another free and fantastic tool that will help you find niche trends before anyone else.

Head to Exploding Topics. You can filter by category and time to find niche ideas.

In the search results, the exploding topics are shown as green ones, and the regular topics are blue. Try to avoid peaked topics which are red since they're probably too competitive already.

This could be a compelling approach to discover profitable ones before they actually explode. Keep an eye on this one.

3. **Trends24**

Trends24 is a website monitoring the last 24h of trends on Twitter. It provides a more effective way than checking on Twitter directly.

You will be able to filter by location, which can be helpful if you prefer to focus on a local niche. This is an easy and straightforward approach to help you find what's trending. Trends' demand on Twitter can be a good reflection of the niche demand on TikTok.

Method #2 Check Google search volume

Finding out how many people are searching for your niche idea is a solid validation approach. It can give you some insights into your niche idea's potential traffic. You can use some paid SEO tools, while here's a free resource for you.

- **Ubbersuggest**

Go to Ubbersuggest, and type your niche idea to search.

Then check the keyword's search volume, which will give you an approximate estimation of search volume by month. Typically, anything above 10k is good.

Scroll down to the keyword ideas section. It provides more data on related search terms. Please note that you are not trying to figure out the competition at this step. You are figuring out whether there's a massive demand for your ideas.

Also, the broader terms, the bigger demand you will want to see.

5. How To Study Your Competitors On TikTok

Now you probably have just a few most promising niche ideas on your list. It's time to study how competitive they are on TikTok to choose the best one. Your goal is to find a more profitable niche idea with less competition. In other words, find niches with lots of views but without many posts, which is a sign of trendy topics on TikTok without much competition.

Head to TikTok, enter your niche idea in the search bar. In the search results, check:

1.   How many TikTokers are dedicated to the same niche idea under the **Users** section? They are your direct competitors.

2.   How many videos with similar topics are already posted under the **Videos** section? They are your indirect competitors.

3.   Go to the **Hashtag** section, check what the sizes of related hashtags are. If there are many big hashtags (with millions or even billions of posts) in this niche, it can mean this niche is in high demand but could be competitive.

Then check the kind of content of your competitors to learn how they attract their audience as well as how they monetize. Pay attention to the following aspects when you study your competitors' content:

- What kind of content do they film about?
- How often do their post?
- How are they engaging with their audience?
- How long are their videos? 15s? 60s? or 3m?
- How do they convert their viewers to followers?
- How do they monetize?
- How possible if you can do better than them?

Content is the main aspect to analyze in your competitors' accounts. They may already have optimized their strategy and are using what works for the best. Why not take advantage of this? Don't forget to create something better. If you can generate better content compared to your competitors, you are more likely to get the audience faster and rank higher on TikTok.

Write all the information you've gathered down. Now, you will have a much better idea of deciding which niche is the best for you.

6. Find Your Own Niche

If you already have perfected your content on other social media platforms, just use your expertise to shoot TikTok content aligning with other presence. This will not only save your time in figuring out your strengths but also allow you to drive your own traffic to your TikTok profile, and your followers probably will continue to follow you on TikTok. Youtuber Skincarebyhyram is a perfect example. He is originally a skincare specialist on YouTube, and now he uses TikTok as another source of sharing his knowledge and passion about skincare.

While if you just start, it's ok too. Follow the above steps to find your own profitable niche. It's also important to pick a TikTok niche that you are interested in, or at least you can tolerate making content every day and for a long time. This is because most successful accounts on TikTok post videos every day, many of them even multiple times per day, even when they don't have much attention.

You do have to be consistent with your followers. Otherwise, they probably won't stick around for too long since so many other influencers are more consistent for them to follow.

If you have broader interests or don't want to focus only on one niche, then make some videos for each niche. Once your TikTok begins to gain traction, you can then narrow your focus down to the videos that have performed the best. You can continue to make similar videos that are engaging your viewers.

If you still have no idea, how about starting by jumping on the latest social challenges and trends? Surely, you can still create content that's on-trend while remember to put your own pin on the challenge to help ensure it aligns with your current feed.

7. Top TikTok Niches

1. Funny Dances

It's easy to notice that dances are probably one of the most popular niches on TikTok. But there are probably millions of "dancers" accounts.

A great alternative is focusing on the funny dances niche to remove many competitors who focus on other dancing styles or are just generic. Considering many people visit TikTok for a laugh, why not providing some original dances?

If you check funny dances trend on Google Trends, you will also observe that funny dances are becoming very popular during the last couple of years.

At the time of writing, if we look for #funnydances hashtags on TikTok, there are 725 funny dances posts with 1.9 million reviews.

The post number is not that high, suggesting it's not that competitive yet. Besides, the overall views are 1.9 million, which is a lot!

Hashtag tip: If you want to try this niche, here are some of the best hashtags for you:

- #funnydances
- #funnydancers

- #funnyvideos

- #funnydance

- #funnydancemoves

- #funnydancevideos

- #funnydancesisters

2. Fitness Fashion

It can work great to mix two popular niches into one sub-niche for more targeted followers. The Fitness Fashion niche is a mix of two popular bigger niches: fitness and fashion, which work very well on TikTok.

On Google Trend, this trend is slowly increasing in popularity because fitness and fashion only began to appear together on platforms recently.

At the time of writing, if we look for # fitnessfashion hashtags on TikTok, there are 748 overall posts with 21.8 million reviews. It's clear that how popular this content is. Compared to the views count, the hundreds of posts suggest there are not many TikTokers focused on this niche yet.

Hashtag tip: The following are some most popular hashtags you can use for this niche:

- #fitness

- #fitnessfashion

- #fitnessmotivation

- #gymwear

- #gym
- #activewear

3. Easy Dinner

Considering TikTok user's demographics, this can be another popular niche. Lots of people look for quick dinner ideas so that they will be able to prepare something effortlessly and fast.

On Google Trend, we can see that easy dinner has a stable trend and a clear increase of Covid-19, which makes it a great opportunity to try this niche.

Currently, the thousands of #easydinner videos have 254.5 million views on TikTok. Taking into the number of views per video, this seems like a demanded niche.

Hashtag tip: some of the best hashtags for this niche are:

- #easydinner
- #easyrecipes
- #food
- #dinner
- #foodie
- #dinnerideas
- #foodporn.

4. Dark Comedy

Without a doubt, comedy is one of the main reasons TikTok users love sticking around this platform. So it makes a lot of sense to take advantage of the comedy niche.

The data on Google Trend shows that it's popular search with a stable trend with a slight increase in the last few years.

If we look for #darkcomedy hashtags on TikTok, it has 8.7 thousand videos with 476.2 million overall views. In this case, the post count is a bit higher, which suggests more competitors. But the views are also much higher.

Hashtag tip: Here are some of the most popular hashtags for this niche:

- #darkcomedy
- #darkhumor
- #comedy
- #satire
- #politicalsatire
- #halloween

5. Funny Memes

Following the last logic, comedy and memes perform very well individually on TikTok. So targeting this niche as a whole will make sense.

The Google Trend also shows us clearly how popular funny memes are, and they have a significant increase in interest recently.

TikTok proves this result. With 87.3 k funny memes are kind of the most competitive niche in our list. Its overall views reached 4.3 billion, suggesting a vast interest in this niche among TikTok users.

Hashtag tip: the most popular hashtags you can use for this niche include:

- #funnymemes
- #funny
- #memes
- #meme
- #memesdaily
- #dankmemes
- #lol

6. Realistic Drawing

Art is another popular niche in many social media platforms. However at is too extensive, so it's advisable to niche down into a popular art one.

On Google Trend, we will see how "realistic drawing" is not only trendy but also is increasing its interest.

Also, with thousands of videos on TikTok, this niche has 131.5 million views. The post count vs. overall views provides a great proportion, which means there is lots of interest in TikTok for this niche while not that many competitors.

Hashtag tip: some of the most popular hashtags you can use:

- #realisticdrawing
- #artist
- #art
- #drawing
- #realism
- #artwork

7. **Street Style**

Similar to other platforms, fashion is probably the largest niche. But the competence is brutal since you will have to compete with big influencers and brands. That's why focusing on a smaller sub-niche like street style could be a good idea.

According to Google Trend, this niche has increased interest in the last few years, which provides a fantastic opportunity for fashion lovers who want a less competitive niche.

If we check this niche on TikTok, the total number of "street style" posts is not too much compared to the overall views (2.2 billion.) This suggests there's an average of 7.3k views per video, which is way above average.

Hashtag tip: the most popular hashtags you can use for this niche include:

- #streetstyle

- #streetwear
- #fashion
- #style
- #streetphotography
- #ootd
8. **Couple Goals**

The relationship niche typically generates interest among users on all platforms. TikTok is not an exception. To be more specific, "couple goals" is one of the most popular niches.

Google Trends also tells us how popular this niche is, with lots of interest over time.

The 150.5 billion reviews show how popular this niche is. So even though this niche could be a good choice, you will still need to make a difference if you want to stand a chance.

Hashtag tip: popular hashtags you can use for this niche include:

- #couplegoals
- #couple
- #love
- #relationshipgoals
- #like
- #couples
- #wedding
9. **Beauty Tips**

This beauty niche is a fool-proof category with many interested users.

Google Trend shows that the interest in beauty tips increased dramatically since 2018 and has been stable since then, which makes it a fantastic niche.

#beautytips has 8.4 billion views at the time of writing, while the competence may be higher than others. Since it still has 57.3k average views per post, it's still worth the effort.

Hashtag tip: Here are some of the most popular hashtags for this niche:

- #beautytips
- #skincare
- #beauty
- #skincareroutine
- #makeup
- #skincaretips
- #beautycare

10. Home Fitness

It's one of the latest trends brought about by the Covid outbreak.

It's clear on Google Trend that home fitness already had a stable trend, and its interest spikes right after Covid.

Hashtag tip: Here are some of the most popular hashtags for this niche:

- #homefitness
- #fitness
- #workout
- #homeworkout

- #homegym
- #fitfam
- #gym

Conclusion

In order to find the best TikTok niche, you need to niche down and look for popular niches among your target audience without lots of competitors. A great and profitable niche should have a balance between popularity and competence.

Choosing the right niche is still the first step. Next is to create quality content daily and tailor it to your target audience.

Ok, now it's your turn!

Section: TikTok Profile Optimization

TikTok is a social media platform providing an amazing opportunity for organic promotions. It's true that every video has the potential to go viral even without spending a single marketing dollar. Plenty of businesses have blown up overnight with one single post.

Before you start investing time in making your TikTok videos, the first step is setting up your profile properly to succeed on this platform. Optimizing your TikTok profile page can help convert your efforts into actual conversions and clicks.

In this section, we will be talking about the killer ways of how you can easily optimize your TikTok profile.

1. Optimize Your TikTok Username

To optimize any social media channel, it's essential to pick an easy-to-remember username. Remember your username is the first word on your profile that's the most important in the eyes of your audience.

It would also be beneficial for you to include the keyword in this field. TikTok has machine-based learning. This means when you use keywords in your username, it will send a signal to the TikTok algorithm about what your content is focusing on.

Also, it can be helpful to have a brandable name that's easy to remember. This is attractive since it represents both your personality and business.

2. Make Your TikTok Profile Photo Stand Out

When a user visits your profile, the first thing they will see is your profile photo. It can be the best place to convince viewers to follow you. However, it's not possible with a bad one.

First, it's strongly recommended to keep the same photo on all your social media accounts: TikTok, Twitter, Instagram, YouTube, LinkedIn, Facebook, Pinterest, etc. Or at least aim for a similar profile photo for all your accounts, making sure all your social media channels have a similar visual match.

Please note that photos must be at least 20*20 pixels.

Tips for Best Profile Photo:

- Instead of showing too much of your body, show your face as your profile picture. Crop to the head and a bit of shoulder.
- When you take a photo, pick a flattering background. Too much clutter in the background will make your photo less appealing.

- Pick a soft light source, and the best bet will be near a window on a sunny day.
- A smiling face always gets more attention. Click a smiling pose. The eye contact will take your photo to the next level.
- To get the best one, try different angles.
- Retouch your profile photo. Every nice picture needs a retouch. You can use some photo retouching apps or software out there or hire a freelancer.

Bonus Tips:

- If you can include some kind of prop, your brand colors, or something speaking to your personality.
- Sketchy profile photo is trending now. It's worth a try if you like this style too.

3. Optimize Your TikTok Bio

Your bio is your chance to introduce your brand and yourself to potential followers. If you have a great bio, you don't have to re-introduce yourself in every video. Take advantage of this to tell your audience who you are and why they should follow you.

Creating a converting bio does not have to be difficult. Here, we'll introduce how you can optimize your TikTok bio to help you grow your following and attract more qualified leads for your business ultimately.

Now, let's dig deeper into these five steps.

1. Describe yourself or your brand

Let your followers know who you are and what you do. They could put together some idea of what your profile is all about from watching your videos. However, you won't want to rely just on this. Sometimes, you want to make a video that's crucial to you but has nothing to do with your brand, and what are you going to do then? Yes, your audience needs another way to learn what your account is about.

It only needs to be a few words, so be sure you can boil down exactly what you like your audience to know before they decide whether to follow you. Also, make your language compelling, engaging, and efficiently get across your brand's purpose and value.

2. Add emojis

An emoji can help you emphasize your brand's personality further. You can notice that lots of TikTok bios have an emoji in them. Emojis will enable you to show your brand's services or products without taking up too much space.

For example, if your company sells video tools, you can include the video camera emoji 📹. If your eCommerce business is selling clothing, you may include a t-shirt emoji 👕.

On the other hand, you can use emojis to tell the audience what to do. For instance, if you want people to hit the follow button or click the link below, you can add arrows to express those without adding extra characters to ask them to take action.

3. Add a Call-To-Action (CTA)

Call-to-action is to tell your audience exactly what to do next, letting them know how to interact with you. For example, you can include a CTA to direct your followers to an eCommerce website, your blog posts, or other social channels like YouTube or Instagram.

You'll want to get in the habit of adding CTAs to almost every piece of communication or content you want to share with your followers. At the very least, ask your audience to follow you on TikTok. This is the most effective way to get them more enticed to take action right away after watching your content.

4. Pay attention to the character limit

The same with other social media platforms, TikTok also has a character limit for their bio. You will only have 80 characters to express yourself, which is just over half of the limit on Instagram. It is kind of tight. While this is another reason that emojis can be super helpful. You want to save your characters and wisely use them to fully communicate yourself or your brand to your audience.

Pick the most vital aspects and highlight them in your TikTok bio.

5. Add a link in your bio

Links are valuable to direct your traffic from TikTok to other pages you want to promote. You may want to direct your audience or followers to a relevant landing page to capture their contact information and gather your email lists or an e-book or sales page for the most recent products you mentioned in your video.

A couple of different ways are available to optimize the link in your TikTok bio. Let's dive into each one.

- **URL**

You can choose to put a link in your bio to send traffic to only a single URL. You may want to drive traffic to your most recent blog post, a dedicated landing page, your homepage, another social media profile, or any other page you want.

You are also able to promote multiple links via a link bio service, such as urlbio or linktree. With their service, you will be able to drive the audience to a single web page with a collection of page links they can visit. You may want to include links to your affiliate links, blogs, products, and other social media sites. This option gives your audience more choices of where to go and the possibility of connecting with you outside of TikTok. It also can save you the hassle of updating your links every time you upload a new post promoting a different service or product. But if you are going to try this route, remember to limit the links included on your link page. If there are too many options within your list, visitors may get overwhelmed and just choose to exit out.

- **Accessing the Link in TikTok Bio**

Not everyone has the ability to add a link to their bio yet. If you want to check whether you have the option, go to "**Edit your profile.**" If you can see a "**website**" option underneath the section, it means you can add a link directly.

If you didn't see that option in your app, don't worry. Here is another way you can add a link: join the TikTok Testers program.

To join the program, go to your app's **Settings and Privacy**, scroll down to the bottom, and you will find it.

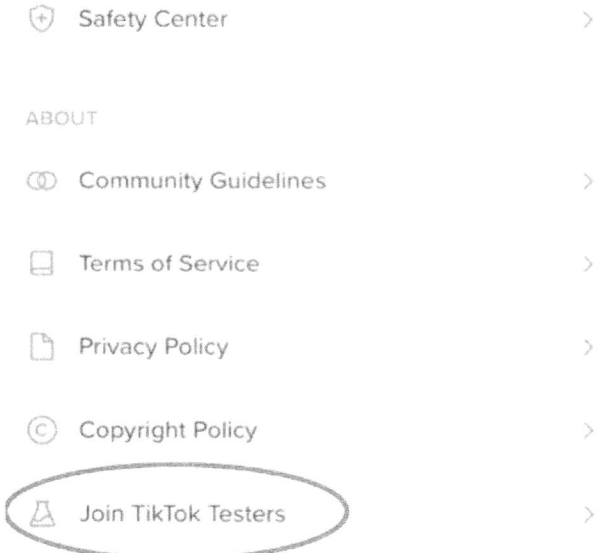

From the instructions from there, you can access the different beta versions as they release them. This program aims to ensure that only the best features are available to the public and keep the app as bug-free as possible.

TikTok Bio Examples

Now you learned all the elements you need for a fully optimized bio. To help you see these strategies in action, let's take a look at several excellent examples.

1. Food

This is something almost everyone loves to see. TikTok users are not the exceptions. One of the internet's most loveable and favorite @foodqood has made quite a name for himself on TikTok.

He shares delicious and cute-looking dessert recipes. We can see that his bio is well-optimized, with a very brief description of who he is, call-to-action emojis, and a link to his own link page, which includes his other social media platforms and merchandise for followers to buy.

2. Travel

Travel is another super popular niche on TikTok. Whether you are sharing interesting things about your hometown or documenting your own travels, there are lots of ways to show travel videos on TikTok.

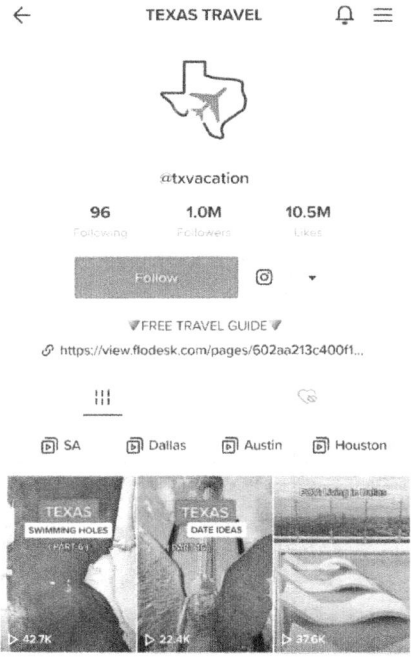

This account, @txvacation, has a great bio, including a brief description, emojis, and a landing page link to build the email list.

3. Fashion

There is no shortage of fashion influencers and people who just love fashion on TikTok.

Here @lifestyle1130 uses his bio to share how to pose when taking pictures in various settings. We can see he has emojis and descriptions of his account's purpose – teaching you how to take nice photos, a call to action with a link to his YouTube channel. He even includes his Q&A page to interact better with his followers.

4.Other TikTok Profile Optimization Tips

1. Insert Your Instagram and Youtube Link

TikTok allows you to link your TikTok account to Instagram and YouTube accounts directly. Don't take it lightly. Once you get popular on TikTok, it will become your No.1 source of more followers on Instagram or YouTube.

If you haven't started other social media platforms,

just get started on YouTube since plenty of TikTokers have already started YouTube and drive their traffic to YouTube in order to monetize their content in more ways.

2. Consider using hashtags

Hashtag plays an important part in TikTok. With the right branded hashtag, the audience interested in your profile could find you easier since the right hashtag can help them easily search and follow you.

3. Switch to a Business account

If you are serious with TikTok, consider converting your account to a business account to get more data and analytics. With a business account, you will be able to check your video views, profile views, followers, and their demographics.

It's also free and easy to switch. Click three dots in the upper-right corner and click "**Manage Account**," you will see "**Switch to Business Account**" under the **Account control** section. You will also be able to choose the category that best describes your account.

Conclusion

As TikTok continues to grow, many influencers and business owners consider it to help them increase their awareness. With more and more opportunities to gain more followers and get more visible, you can easily optimize your TikTok profile by following the above ways.

So, you don't have to miss out on this great movement. Now it's time to open your TikTok and start or update your profile.

Section: TikTok Algorithm & Metrics

1. Use TikTok Algorithm To Your Advantage

The TikTok algorithm may seem mysterious and complicated. From what hashtags you use, music choices, your location, to even the first video you liked on TikTok, they all can affect the algorithm. In this section, we'll decode everything we've learned about the TikTok algorithm as well as how you are able to start using it to your own advantage.

1.1 How TikTok Algorithm Works

According to TikTok: "Our system recommends users' content by ranking videos based on a combination of factors, such as the interests you express as our new user. We will adjust for things you show that you are not interested in."

We can see that the algorithms of For You Page are based on users' preferences and their activity history. In other words, because of the sheer number of variations and factors involved, no two For You Feeds will be exactly the same. Your recommendations will be carefully curated for you.

The factors affecting the recommendations include:

- **User interactions**

It's easy to understand that user activity plays a crucial role in determining which videos TikTok presents. Below are the most critical factors:

- Content created
- Video shares
- Video likes
- Comments posted
- Accounts followed

The algorithm also considers how far a user got in your video and whether they watched it to the end. If a user watches a video from beginning to end, it's a strong sign of interest. The completion rate carries a greater weight in the TikTok algorithm compared to some other contributing factors.

Also, showing up in TikTokers' feeds regularly goes beyond only being a follower. Compared to the TikTokers they simply follow but scroll past, users will be shown more content from TikTokers that they engage with.

- **Video information**
  - Captions
  - Length/runtime
  - Hashtags
  - Sounds
  - Stickers

Hashtags, especially, are the main component of which videos will be recommended. Users who create or watch a video with a specific hashtag will be more likely to see the videos with that hashtag later.

- **Device and account settings**

TikTok does take these settings into consideration, but it also clarifies that they are not given as much weight as other factors. Example factors of device and account settings include:

- o Language preference
- o Device type
- o Country setting

These factors are used to make sure the system is optimized for performance.

1.2 What Doesn't Affect The "For You" Feed

Based on the functionality of the For You algorithm, the number of total followers TikTok accounts have doesn't make their videos rank higher or be shown more often. Naturally, the accounts with more followers will have more overall visibility, but their videos aren't given preferential treatment. This means that a video from a TikTok with more followers or/and a history of high-performing videos won't get recommended more often compared to a video from a new TikToker with fewer followers or/and lower-performing videos.

This is to say that videos are measured and recommended based on their own merits instead of their creators' merits.

1.3 How TikTok Calculates Effect

Even though TikTok has shared some information about algorithmic functions, they didn't share everything and left some answers to the anecdotal speculation.

You may have heard of the **batch effect,** which is a popular theory among creators of TikTok. According to this theory, TikTok basically shows your video to different batches of random users at different times. How these users react will determine whether your video will get shared with more people. Essentially, the more interactions and views your video gets, the greater number of "batches" see it down the line.

In addition, the time lags between different batches sometimes can take up to a number of days. Many creators have observed that their video views "jump" significantly after plateauing, which is speculated to be thanks to the next "batch" launched, and their videos have been exposed to more viewers.

TikTok Effects & Filters

Effects and filters are used to make your content more engaging and compelling for the audience. TikTok provides brands and content creators a wide variety to choose from and releases new options regularly. Its filters and effects are a significant part of what sets TikTok apart from its competitors, such as Instagram Reels.

Plenty of analysts have noted that TikTok seems to prioritize videos that use its effects, especially the filters or effects that are currently trending.

1.4 The Cycle to Go Viral on TikTok

As we introduced above, TikTok typically pushes your video to a random group of users. This is known as the initial push. Then the algorithm calculates the video's performance and decides the next steps. The base of the performance evaluation is the engagement metrics. Even though lots of users speculate on which metrics are more important, no one knows what the actual criteria are. Generally speaking, it seems that its algorithm favors the re-watch rate and the shares over likes.

Also, after the initial push, the TikTok algorithm looks for users who are more likely to engage with your content. There is another theory, saying that TikTok creates tribes of users with similar affinities and interests. Its algorithm will use the data gathered from the initial push to decide which tribes your video may do better with.

In the next section, we will introduce detailed strategies for making your content go viral.

1.5 A commonly Asked Video Flop Question Answered

Plenty of TikTokers have asked the same question: if a video flopped today, will it get views again tomorrow?

Flop is a term commonly used by TikTok content creators to describe a video that hasn't received any substantial reviews.

And the answer to that question is YES. This is unlike other social media platforms. TikTok's algorithm could begin pushing a video several weeks before, even if it has flopped after the initial push. This tells us the importance of sticking to a specific niche as well as avoiding deleting any of your previous videos.

As a video goes viral, lots of viewers will also visit the profile of the video's creator and watch those older videos. So if the creator has stuck to a specific niche, they're more likely to get viewers to engage with their older videos too. At the same time, TikTok detects the new engagement with the older content and will serve them to other similar viewers as well.

2. TikTok Metrics You Should Track

Influencer marketing is one of the most effective strategies a content creator or a brand can adopt in the social media age. TikTok analytics are key to step up your TikTok strategy. What you need is a free business account to take advantage of them. You will be able to really understand what your target audiences are interested in with the TikTok built-in analytics. Now, we are breaking down the TikTok business analytics and how those metrics will help you grow your business.

To get TikTok analytics, we need to switch our account into a business one. In the TikTok Profile Optimization Section, we've introduced how to switch to a business account. Once you did the switch, go to **Creator tools** under the **settings and privacy**. Then you will see **Analytics**. There are three tabs in the Analytics: Overview, Content & Followers.

2.1 Understand TikTok metrics:

Dashboard #1: Overview

- **Video views**

This is the number one metric you need to follow. It shows the total number of views your videos were watched. If you just started, upload videos with different formats and study which types can get more views to build your TikTok marketing strategy better. The views are public-facing, and you can easily benchmark your views against your competitors.

- **Profile views**

Another metric that can track if you want to be seen out there. You are able to see how many people have clicked through your profile. Also, compare this to the number of video views you received. Calculate what percentage of people are interested in your content enough to click through your profile. It's vital to track the relationship between profile and video views for moving viewers down the marketing funnel.

- **Likes, comments & shares**

Shares are also a good indicator to tell if your content is able to reach a broader audience.

Comments function like a validation that you have been doing a great job. When someone stops at your video and leaves a comment, make sure that audience will return to your profile soon.

The number of shares, likes, and comments per video is going to help you get a clear idea of how your videos are resonating with those who saw them. Just like you can with Instagram, you can use these metrics to calculate engagement rates.

Dashboard #2: Content

- **Trending videos**

TikTok built-in analytics can calculate which of your videos have the fastest growth in view count. With this information, you are able to assess which types of content are with the biggest potential to go viral.

Dashboard #3: Followers

This is a great place to learn about your followers. So make this section a good source for your content inspiration.

- **Followers**

This will show you the number of followers you gained or lost each week. If you see this number drop, you should change your strategy since it means your content doesn't bring new followers.

- **Top territories**

This shows the followers' distribution by territory. It will tell you where your followers are located by country as a percentage breakdown. Keep these places in mind since it makes sense to localize your content and future promotions.

- **Gender**

You will see your followers' distribution by gender. It can help you understand your followers better and create different content. If you are happy with your niche, continue playing with your crowd. While if you want to grow your audience, think about creating content with more universal appeal. Another way is to partner with a relevant influencer to get exposure with a different group of users.

- **Followers activity**

It's a super helpful metric that shows not only the exact dates and frequent times your audiences are active but also the times your viewers are the least active. Try to post regularly in the time slot when activity is consistently high.

- **Sounds your followers have listened to**

You can use this information to make the best strategy. Now you know what sounds your followers are interested in, all you need to do is grabbing your phone and begin filming. Also, make sure you save those songs to your **Favorites** for later use. (Just tap on the song, then press the bookmark icon.)

Please note since trends move fast on TikTok, plan for a fast turnaround.

- **Videos your followers watched**

You can see which videos are popular among your followers. It can help you figure out what your followers want to see, and you can replicate that type of content more. It's also a great place to scope out potential collaborators.

2.2 Metrics for an individual post

You are also allowed to see your analytics for an individual post. Simply tap on the video's thumbnail, and you will see its unique dashboard. The metrics you can get include:

- o Total video views;
- o Total like count of your post;
- o Total shares on your video;
- o Total number of comments;
- o **Total playtime**: This stat doesn't reveal much on its own. However, you can compare it with other posts to decide your account's average total playtime.
- o **Average watch time**: This can give you a good indication of how successful you are at maintaining your audience's attention.
- o **Traffic source types**: Traffic sources include your profile, For You feed, following feed, searches, sounds, and hashtags.

- ○ **Audience territories**: if you created a campaign or post for a specific location, here is where you can see if it has reached them.

2.3 TikTok Analytics Reporting

Now, you are an expert at TikTok analytics. It's time for you to assess your performance. Keep track of your videos and sounds your audience watched the most on a weekly basis.

Pro tip: TikTok analytics only show data for 28 days before expiring. Regularly check in to report your progress to avoid missing out. This is not only a great source of inspiration but also a place for you to discover popular sounds, themes, hashtags to use in your upcoming TikTok content.

3. TikTok Engagement Rates

There are different ways to calculate engagement rates on social media. TikTok is no different. Here are two primary formulas you can use:

1) ((likes number + comments number) / Followers number) * 100
2) ((likes number + comments number + shares number) / Followers number) * 100

Because comment and like metrics are visible on TikTok, you can easily see how your TikTok metrics compare with other accounts. You are also better to scope out the engagement rates of influencers before teaming up with them.

Average engagement estimate

If you want to know the back-of-the-envelope estimate of any account's average engagement, here is how:

1. Go to that profile, click **Likes** to get the complete total
2. Count the posted videos' number
3. Then divide likes by the videos' number
4. Next, divide this number by that account's total followers' number
5. Last, multiply by 100.

Please note that most engagement rate formulas include comments and likes, so you should not compare this result with those calculations. However, because it's time-consuming to count all comments, this formula can be used as a fast way to compare accounts in-house.

Conclusion

TikTok is a social media platform where the potential to go viral can skyrocket your business's engagement and reach. Monitor these right metrics over time and use them to improve your campaigns continuously. You will be able to develop a presence on this app before your competitors and help your account or brand find a significant ROI (return on investment) on this hottest new social media platform.

Section: Influencer Strategy: TikTok SEO

Part of what makes TikTok so fun is that any type of content has a chance to succeed on this platform. A viral or successful video can bring you much more attention and followers as well as make it easier for you to monetize this traffic later.

Before we start, the first thing you need to know is that TikTok is a meritocracy giving every video a chance by showing it to a small audience on the For You Page, even if you have zero followers. At this test stage, If your video performs well with this small group, TikTok then will continue to push it out to more and more people who probably will like it. So typically, you will be able to tell in the first hour or two if you just created a viral video.

So how can you make contents go viral on TikTok and gain lots of attention?

1. How To Create Viral TikTok Video

1. Kick your video off using a strong opening hook or bang – the 3-second rule

TikTok is a fast-paced social media platform where you need to grab your audience's attention in the first few seconds. To make your video perform well, you have to catch their attention fast before they swipe past your post to check other content.

It's vital to hook your audience early to make them watch till the very end. Set the topic and tone of your video within the first 3 seconds to let people understand what they are watching. In this way, TikTok will be very likely to feature your video and more and more audience.

Based on your own niche and content, there are various ways to capture your target audience's attention right away. You will need to experiment here and there to figure out what works the best for you. For example, posing a staggering question can be a strong hook, or you can try to tell your audience what your video will be about by putting a unique spin on it or tell your viewers to stop scrolling.

2. Keep your video as engaging and short as possible

TikTok is still a short video media platform where the viewers prefer to watch clips that are to the point and short.

TikTok will look at the average length of watch time compared to the video length as a way to evaluate the video's quality. You want your audience to watch your video from start to end, which makes your completion rate reach 100%. It's much more likely to have viewers finish 8 seconds of a 10-second video compared to 48 seconds of a 1-minute one.

What if you do have a lengthy story to tell? Then

break it into several parts. But remember to remind your followers to follow and like for part 2 and so on. You can also turn the entire topic into a video series, making the topic in more depth.

Keep in mind that as your TikTok completion rate increases, so will your chance to go viral on TikTok.

3. User voiceover

TikTok wants to show your videos to the right viewers and use all the methods you provided to learn what your videos are about and push them to the proper viewers. Of course, you can do this in your hashtags and captions, which we will elaborate on later. However, using a voiceover on your video will give TikTok significantly more information and keywords on your video for them to be able to show your videos to the right viewers.

4. Use trending sounds or music

Consider music like hashtags on TikTok. They play an important role in your videos' discoverability. TikTok is a social platform where users feed off the trends, so it can help boost your chances of getting your content to go viral by using current trending songs.

How to find trending and popular songs? You will need to begin paying attention to the popular artists and creators to see what is actually working. Another way is to consume the videos on your "For You Page," and you will notice what sounds and music are getting the most traction right now. After finding the trending sound that you want to use, you can save it at your favorites for later use.

One more way for you. Click the "Add sound" at the top when you film your video. Then you will be able to scroll through those trending songs under the **Discover** section.

Pro tip: Even if you are doing a voiceover, you can still use trending music in your videos. To do this, just turn the volume all the way to zero or layer the sound quietly in the video's background. Keep in mind that those songs function like hashtags.

5.   Master the art of storytelling

It's a crucial part of humanity. The audience will be more likely to share videos that can capture their emotions. You will have a better chance to capture the audience's attention by adding raw human emotions like fear, humor, inspiration, and excitement because they can connect with your stories.

Yes, dances do well on the app. But let's be real, unless you are a talented dancer or a hilariously bad one, your dance videos will not be likely to go viral easily on TikTok. For us regular people who are not blessed by the gods of rhythm, we have a better chance to go viral by telling a compelling and interesting story. Your stories can be anything. It can be something random that happened during your day, something interesting happened, a project you did, or anything else. Just keep your plots flowing fast.

Pro tip: use text overlays when telling a story to capture your audience's attention. For example, you can try to add a fear right off the bat, followed by step by step, and provide a solution in the end. Or try to tell a story while leaving some cliffhangers that can promote some comments and engagement on your video.

6. Share advice, tips, or favorite things

Users also love learning on this platform. If you have some expertise in a certain field, make some informational videos to help others learn more about it. In this case, quick bullet point videos can work well. Also, you can use some texts over the screen guiding your audience through your mini-lesson.

On the other hand, people also love shopping on TikTok, so sharing your favorite products will be a surprisingly easy way to gain lots of traction as well as monetize.

7. Don't be afraid of being different and do something slightly controversial

There are lots of TikTok videos that went viral because their creators have tried new things out of the norm. Users are used to watching similar types of content on Tiktok. If you can try something unique, unexpected, or different on a certain topic, you will reach virality easier on this platform.

This is because commenting drives virality and people love to give their two cents on things over the internet. Actually, you don't need to do anything wrong. While if there's a topic that people are divided on, such as is ketchup on eggs acceptable, how much cream cheese is right on a bagel (literally this kind of small silly thing!), people love to jump in and comment on them.

So if you decided to go on the slightly controversial route, you should promote high engagement in your comment section. At the end of the day, embrace your haters since they are the ones who help you go viral on TikTok.

8. Always have a strong call to action

This is probably the most important strategy that not only can help your videos go viral but also help you grow your followers. Remember, going viral is NOT your ultimate goal. You want to encourage your audience to follow your profile, like and comment on your videos, go to your website, check the services or products you are promoting, etc. You can simply add "follow for more," "like for part 2," or "don't let this flop."

Pro tip: It's advisable to have your CTA at least several seconds long, allowing people to have time to follow you before they move to the next one.

9. Make your video that some parts of it need to be rewatched

As mentioned, your video's completion rate is

super helpful for the algorithm. This may sound counterintuitive. It can be helpful for your videos to go viral by having some parts where are too fast for the audience to watch, read, or understand on their first view. For example, put an important address, statement, or a list of places for just one second. Some interested audience will be very likely to pause or rewatch your video to catch that information. When they do this, they are spending more time watching your video, which sends a signal to the TikTok algorithm that your video is good, and TikTok will show your video to more and more people. This is when your video is going viral.

You even can put "pause to read" on a certain point in your video, for 1-1.5 seconds at most. Similar to have a CTA, when you actually tell your audience what to do, they will be more likely to follow the instructions.

10. Include random details for the audience to comment on

You will find that people love commenting on the random things in the TikTok video, and they love spotting little details that are not even the major points of the video. The more comments you can get, the more likely your video can go viral. For example, wear some weird or cool in your video, and many people will ask where it's from. Remember, you can do this in so many different approaches.

11. Leave some unanswered questions

This is another way to get comments. When you post a video, you can take time to think of an obvious question that the audience will have. Do not explain it, which could lead to lots of comments and help your videos do well.

12. Reply to all your comments

This is similar to other social media platforms: it's smart to reply to all your comments. If you can engage with your commenters, they will get more motivated to continue commenting on your videos.

Pro tip: reply to the comments with another related question to keep your conversation going. Also, don't go too fast, or you'll probably get blocked.

You also can reply to a comment with a video for more context and greater engagement.

13. Be fast to hop on the trend wave

If you want your video to go viral, go and spot the trends before other people. You will stay ahead of the trend wave and avoid the later fierce competition.

One straightforward way is to check out TikTok's Discovery page. If you spot a trending video related to your niche, it's time to put your own unique twists and catch the trend.

Some trends are seasonal, and some are spontaneous. So it's best to spot the trends which will be effective in your niche or expertise and be fast to leverage them before fading.

14. Be authentic and original

If you can create funny, meaningful, or interesting original content, this is the best approach to grow your TikTok account. Use a sound or song you created, start your own trend, and share something new. At the same time, make sure to make your videos engaging.

15. If you want to talk about a specific product, avoid linking it right away

When you are trying to monetize your video through an affiliate link or doing a product review, it's understandable to get tempted to drop the product link in the comment immediately. But if you don't drop the link, people are more likely to commenting asking for the link or asking where it's from, which can help your video gain traction in turn.

16. Spend at least 15-30 mins/day watching videos on your FYP

I know you just want to be efficient and come to TikTok only when you post your videos. While it's crucial to spend a little every day watching videos on your FYP, especially if you just start. It can help you get new ideas and be updated with the current trends, and this is what you will need to create top-performing content.

17. Post frequently

It's still kind of a number game to go viral on TikTok. The more often you post, the higher chance you will have a video go viral. While don't skimp on quality. If you push yourself to push out videos consistently, not only will your videos' quality get better, but also you're more likely to have one of them go viral on TikTok.

18. Make friends and collaborate with other content creators

It's always beneficial to make friends with other content creators and influencers. It's like the Hype House to have a big group of friends from the same platform. This is not to use your friendship to go viral, but your friends' audiences will likely check you out if you collaborate for a TikTok with them.

Pro tip: Try to make friends with the creators who don't share the same viewers with you. For example, if you are a singer, then collaborate with a dancer or an actor. If you are a comedian, then collaborate with a science guy. This can expand your avenues and bring you more visibility, then go viral.

19. Share your TikTok videos on other social media platforms

If you have other social media platforms, take advantage of them. Upload your TikTok videos to your other social media platforms to get noticed. The audience who watch your content on other platforms will probably check your TikTok profile if they have a TikTok account too, and start following you there. They may also share your videos on their social media, and you will get more views.

20. Incite "FOMO" in the audience

This hack can be best described by the feeling that you will get when a new product comes out and all of your peers get one except you. FOMO is fear of missing out on something that's very amazing or exciting.

If you can create a similar TikTok scenario, users will be encouraged to try your service or product, replicate your content, or join a trend you just created. A great example comes from Little Moons, a mochi ice cream brand that went viral on TikTok. They received a 700% sales surges at Tesco stores! They created a curiosity about their new products and made users feel compelled to test them for themselves. It has bred a big FOMO experience around the products, intrigued users, and peaked their interest.

Conclusion

There's no single foolproof way to go viral. All these strategies apply differently for different audiences. What works for someone else may not work for you. Be flexible and try to have fun creating TikTok videos.

It may take some days, weeks, or even months before you finally find out what works for you. Even if your videos don't go viral quickly, never give up. It's important to know your audience and make contents that can drive engagement and gain more attention. Remember, the potential is limitless. With so many users on TikTok now, content creators and brands will always find more and more ways to innovate for going viral. Arm yourself with the above best tips, and you are going to see progress slowly but surely.

Let's not sleep on TikTok and start with your best content ASAP!

2. How to Find the Best Hashtags for Your Content

There's a hot discussion about TikTok hashtags and their connection to the ever-so-secret TikTok algorithm. Yes, hashtags play a vital role in helping you get noticed on TikTok.

If you want more visibility and reach, you need a solid hashtag strategy. It will also help you identify potential collaborators and competitors and even give you excellent TikTok content ideas.

Now, let's get into the good stuff.

2.1 Hashtags That are Best-performing & Will Get You On FYP Page

1. **Find a balance between niche and broad hashtags**

How broad or niche you should go with your hashtags may be the most challenging part of using hashtags.

On the one hand, it's advisable to get specific with your hashtags, but it's never a good idea to go too niche. Keep in mind that hashtags are all about what the audience is actually searching for.

Before you pick your hashtags, think: would your audience actually type this into the TikTok search bar?

Begin broad and work your way to more specific hashtags. For instance, if you are a marketing professional, #marketing can be your broad hashtag. Depending on your video content, go more niche. For example, your additional hashtags can be #socialmediamarketing or a more specific one - #instagrammarketing.

This is all about finding that perfect balance. As mentioned, finding the secret sauce working the best for you will be a game of trial and error.

2. Discover trending/viral TikTok hashtags

Another great thing about TikTok is that it's easy to discover trending and new hashtags.

To do this, go to the TikTok's discover tab. There, you can scroll through and check what's trending.

You can also simply type in # and let TikTok generate suggestions. Yes, they have a built-in hashtag generator! Those trending and branded hashtags will pop up first, often with a small fire emoji next to them. You need to understand that brands pay lots of money to get those hashtags trending, which means those hashtags have a better chance of being promoted more on the FYP so that TikTok can impress those brands with high impression counts.

Pro tip: jump on trending TikTok hashtags the day/right now they go viral is another handy trick to get more views and reach.

3. Research your competitors and industry leaders

If you are currently low on inspiration, looking at what other industry leaders are doing is one of the best places to begin. If they're working well for them, the chances they will work well for you as well.

If you found the hashtags they are using make sense for your content, take notes of those hashtags.

Also, check your competitors, and look at what's working well for them. Ask yourself the following questions in your research stage to help you build your TikTok hashtag list:

- o Are their hashtags relevant?
- o Did their videos go viral?
- o Is their audience engaging with their content?
- o Did they miss key hashtag opportunities?

4. Find related TikTok hashtags

This is an effective and easy way to grow your community. To find related TikTok hashtags, simply type your hashtags into your TikTok search bar.

Pro tip: leave out the # (hashtag) in your search. Choose "**Hashtag**" under the search bar, and you will be able to see how many views that specific hashtag has. Those numbers are helpful in deciding which one to use.

5. Test

It's all about trial and error. Testing your hashtags on TikTok is vital. Record which ones you used on each of your videos. Also, monitor how many views they are getting overtime. Different hashtags are going to work for different types of videos. Keep trying to find those hashtags that work wonders for your own content.

Pro tip: Consider hashtags like your videos' keywords. So make sure they are clear, relevant, and easily searchable.

2.2 Dummy-proof Hashtag formula

Here is my TikTok hashtag strategy that you can steal to use on your own videos.

The hashtag combo formula:

Broad description hashtags + niche description hastags + location-based hashtags+ trending/viral hashtags.

We've discussed the last trending/viral hashtags in the previous part. Let's talk more about the first three in this section.

- **Broad description hashtags**

The number of hashtags you can use on any post depends on how long your caption is. Typically, it can range between 2-5 hashtags.

First, pick 1-2 descriptive hashtags. For instance, if your videos are about stock trading, then you want to use #stocktrading.

This is the opposite of Instagram, where those popular hashtags actually will limit your reach because there are too many posts for users to see yours. On TikTok, #stocktrading will tell TikTok what your video is about, and they will push your videos to users who are interested in stock trading.

- **Niche description hashtags**

Pick at least one niche hashtag. Let's use the stock trading example. Maybe your trading style is day trading. So use #daytrading to narrow down the topic of your videos even more. By doing this, TikTok will present your videos to users who are not only interested in stock trading but like day trading.

The users who watch your videos will be more likely to like your videos, share them, and comment on them. This will tell TikTok that your videos are great, and TikTok will show them to more people on the For You Page.

- **Location-based hashtag**

Most videos benefit from this type of hashtag. For instance, if your video is about a popular spot to visit in New York City, then use #NYC to let TikTok serve your video to the users who live in NYC since there will probably like your video. If your video is about three dresses to wear at New York Fashion Week, you will also want to use the year's fashion week hashtags, such as #nycfashionweek.

2.3 How Many TikTok Hashtags Should You Use

When deciding how many hashtags you should use in your posts, there is no set rule. However, remember that the longer your hashtags and captions, the more your videos will be obstructed from views.

The TikTok captions have a 100-character limitation, which includes hashtags. So be sure to take advantage of every character. Keep your captions concise to leave room for the important hashtags.

There is no hard rule. Some TikTokers use 1-3 hashtags, while others are using 5-8. It's completely up to you how many hashtags you use. But please do choose your hashtags wisely.

2.4 Take Your TikTok Marketing to the Next Level – Create Your Own Hashtags

Using established hashtags is crucial to increase visibility, while creating your own hashtags will take your TikTok marketing to the next level. Your own branded hashtags will help you stand out in the crowd and offer you the opportunity to get tons of free user-generated content, helping your campaign go viral.

Tips for Creating Your Branded Hashtag

o Your hashtag should be relevant to your product, challenge, campaign, or whatever you are creating the hashtag for.

o Always focus on creating only one hashtag for one campaign rather than creating several ones. This is because others probably will not always copy all your hashtags but will remember to use the major one for sure.

o Create a hashtag with a simple spelling that is easy to remember and without the need to copy & paste. The easier the hashtag to use, the more people will use it.

o Your hashtag should also be self-explanatory, telling people what your content is all about.

o Create a new hashtag for different campaigns or content series to better organize and properly track your content.

Now you have everything you need to know about TikTok hashtags. Apply these hashtag strategies to your advantage. Also, keep in mind that TikTok is all about trial and error. Don't get defeated easily!

3. When Is the Best Time To Post Videos on TikTok

While the content itself and the hashtags you use determine a lot about how much attention you will get, there are a few other factors to consider: timing is a large one. Every platform is unique regarding what performs best, and TikTok is no exception.

As always, the full answer is that it depends on your audience.

According to Influencer Marketing Hub, they have found that the best time to post varies a lot each day during the week by analyzing 10,000 TikTok posts and rates of engagement globally. Based on their result, the best posting times hardly overlap from one day to the next.

Therefore, without a hard scientific conclusion, you need some practical thinking about when your viewers will most likely see your posts. Users tend to skew young, and adults' schedules are different from those of teens.

Two questions to consider:

- ○ **Where are your viewers based?** Figure out where your biggest group of audience is located and their time zone.

- ○ **What is your viewers' schedule?** When do they typically check their phones? The last thing before sleep or the first thing in the morning? When are they out of school? Or on a lunch break? Etc.

Also, the **Tiktok analytics** of business/pro accounts can be super helpful. You will be able to see where your followers come from under the "**Followers**" tab.

If you don't have enough followers data to analyze or just started, here are some general best times to post on TikTok for getting more engagement:

- ○ Mondays: 6 to 10 AM, 10 PM

- ○ Tuesdays: 2 to 4 AM, 9 AM

- ○ Wednesdays: 7 to 8 AM, 11 PM

- ○ Thursdays: 9 AM, 12 to 7 PM

- ○ Fridays: 11 AM, 7 to 8 PM

- ○ Saturdays: 7 to 8 AM, 4 PM

4. How to Get More TikTok Followers

We've talked about how to find your own profitable niche, perfectly set up your profile, make viral videos, and how to use hashtags to your advantage. Those strategies will make your TikTok account reach more people and grow your followers organically.

But reaching millions of people can still be a challenge that will require lots of efforts, planning, and creativity. Like other platforms, TikTok also can help you become an online celebrity with hundreds of thousands of followers. To help your dream come true, besides what we've introduced, we're going to talk about additional strategies for getting more followers. Let's get to the tips!

1. Properly identify your target audience

Each group of age will interact in their ways on TikTok. If you really want to increase your follower numbers on it, you need to know that each niche is different, and there's a wide range of content catering to all niches and groups of ages. So, there's room for everyone.

But, you won't be able to satisfy everyone. It gets vital to know your target audience and make videos that can cater to their unique needs.

Start with thinking about what kind of content your viewers like. For example, if your target viewers are between 13 and 25 years old, you need to create more funny and engaging videos. While if your target viewers are over 35 years old, create more specialized content, which provides them previous advice and educates your followers.

Indeed, you should throw some of your products or services in the mix and make videos showing your audience how you are able to help solve their problems.

2. Always try new TikTok features

Whenever You see TikTok come out with a brand-new feature, go for it. When you use the new feature, TikTok is going to push your videos out even more in return, which helps you reach more potential followers.

3. Follow and unfollow those most popular musers

This is an effective and simple approach to get more attention from those most influential users on TikTok. Find out the most successful Musers in your niche. Then follow and unfollow them until they follow you back. Even though this may seem silly, it actually works. Since after enough attempts, they will probably look at your profile. If they like it, they probably will follow you back.

Also, like and comment on their videos. This is because TikTok will star share on their profiles and increase your chance of being followed back potentially, especially if your comments are always on point. Some of them may even be willing to share their secrets to help you get more followers.

4. Create your own TikTok challenges

If the current trends don't fit your brand's message, creating your own trend is another way to grow your following.

Popular performers such as Jennifer Lopes use TikTok to create challenges where her fans can create videos dancing on her songs and share on TikTok with a certain tag.

On the other hand, brands also get in on the action! Chipotle has created a unique challenge that is easily accessible to all users and stimulates them to have fun. Their **#GuacDance** challenge currently has more than 1 billion views, and **#ChipotleLidFlip** has over 320 million views. This has proven that a fun challenge can be one of the best techniques to grow your following.

5. Repost TikTok as UGC

Because people love to see their content reposted, capitalizing on User-generated content (UGC) will help you get more followers.

It's straightforward to download and repost content from TikTok directly. There are never any issues regarding giving credit since TikTok's logo and creators' handle will automatically be added to each downloaded video.

When you're busy and don't have time to make your own content, reposting UGC will also help you make your TikTok profile "full" by boosting your posting frequency.

Usually, when people know they are featured on an account other than their own, they will get excited to make more and tag the account to have a shot at their followers to check the post.

For example, NARS Cosmetics started reposting UGC content featuring its products, which works for their feed very well. If you are a brand with a physical product, try repost UGC to get more followers.

6. Engage with other TikTokers and content you love

Don't forget TikTok is a social media platform. If you see a video you like, don't forget to leave a comment. The best way to engage with others is by commenting, but try not to be spammy. Try to engage with videos from other influencers, and build a solid network in your niche.

You are going to notice that you have more followers just because you engage with the random videos you love.

7. Create stitchable content

Make TikTok content that can lend itself to being stitched. In other words, you create content allowing other creators to take a bite-sized piece of it.

For example, in your video, you can ask your audience, "tell me you are a music lover without telling me you are a music lover." Other TikTokers will then take the first part of your video, cut this part, and add their content.

Their followers will see your content in their video, and they can see your name is clickable. As those viewers visiting your profile, you will possibly gain lots of new followers just from a small stitched video.

8. Make a video series

Make a series of videos on Tiktok appealing to your audience. For example, if you are a professional organizer, your first video can show viewers how to organize their homes and introduce it as part 1 of the series. By doing so, you give your viewers a reason to come back to see the second one. Some users may happen to see the 3rd video first, and they will go to your profile to watch parts 1 and 2. Now your viewers are binge-watching, and you will end up with a new follower.

Pro tip: make sure you actually tell people directly that it's the 1st, 2nd, 3rd, and so on in your series, so they know to come back to watch other parts.

9. Invite a second person in your TikTok video

Invite a second person in your video will add an element of intrigue, especially if that person only stands there. People will keep watching and anticipate what he/she is going to do. If you pique their interest, they will watch all the way to the end, trying to find out. If you have a pet, like a cat or a dog, include it in the video and test.

10. Go lively Daily

If you have at least 1,000 followers, take advantage of TikTok Live. Live streaming offers you an opportunity to connect with your TikTok community. It allows you to have a back-and-forth conversation with your audience, which you cannot do with your regular videos.

Post a TikTok video before you actually hit the Live button. The visibility of your live stream can help boost your video views.

Pro tip: When you are working, go live. Many people like to get behind the scenes. It's also a fantastic way to build anticipation for the things you are working on. For instance, if you are going to start a podcast, tell your audience what you have lined out for your next episode. Those interested viewers probably will follow you on the podcast too. Now, you not only get more followers on TikTok but also grow your following on other platforms.

11. Explore TikTok paid options

Currently, TikTok ads are still at the infancy stage, meaning the competition is still relatively low. You can use TikTok Ads to target specific demographics and locations, making sure your videos reach the most relevant audiences. This can bring you many conversions into new followers.

Here are four TikTok Ads options:

- **TopView**: shows your profile when TikTok app opens. Since it's one of the first things users will see, this will help you reach a wider audience.

- **In-Feed Ads**: show your content in a user's feed, between the organic posts.

- **Brand Hashtag challenges**: your custom hashtag challenge will be placed on the Discovery page, offering the opportunity for maximum engagement and reach.

- **Brand Takeover**: this is similar to TopView. They are full-screen ads that are shown when users first open the app.

We're expecting to see more options as TikTok Add is still growing.

5.Shortcuts To Accelerate Your TikTok Account Growth

No one will be unhappy when they see their flowers increase. That is closer to their dreams of becoming well-known TikTok influencers. So lots of TikTokers begin to look for the quickest way of getting free followers on TikTok.

Here are several tools that can help you achieve your goal.

- **Social Buddy**

It uses advanced targeting to help you find the followers who are interested in your content. You are able to target potential followers based on niche, industry, complementary accounts, competitors, and relevant hashtags to find your target audience. They focus on getting genuine followers, not fake accounts or bots.

- **Social Viral**

It allows TikTokers to buy followers, likes, and views at a low rate. Social Viral increases your chances of going viral so that you can bring in even more targeted audiences and followers that you don't have to pay for.

- **TikFans**

It is one of the biggest TikTok global communities, providing TikTokers the opportunity of helping each other to boost accounts in various aspects, including getting free followers and likes. More importantly, it's 100% free.

- **FeedPixel**

It is a social media management platform. TikTok creators are able to use it to get more views, likes, and followers. You don't need to provide them with your password or login credentials.

- **InstaFollowers**

This is a tool that can deliver free followers to your account instantly. You also can try to buy them too for this platform too. InstaFollowers provide real and active users with low prices.

It's understandable that these shortcuts are really attractive. But please note that every coin has two sides. Did you think about the engagement rate of your videos if your followers are not real? For the long-term benefits, I still suggest you to try other strategies mentioned here to skyrocket growth on TikTok.

Conclusion

TikTok is a great way to grow your online following. It may be easier to use compared to other platforms, but it still requires strategy. We've introduced many to help you accelerate your account growth.

To become a TikTok influencer, you should know what you are good at. Try to leverage your passions and strengths and create content that can attract attention.

Your style also should be different for people to find and choose to follow you in the crowd of TikTok influencers. Just decide on your forte and go ahead with whatever you believe you can do differently.

Ultimately, the best way to grow your TikTok account will come down to your own creativity. Don't hold back and begin experimenting with the videos you always want to try.

Just do your unique thing, and there are people who will love you.

Section: Master Influencer marketing - How To Drive Traffic & Sales from TikTok

TikTok can be a super powerful way to drive your brand's engagement and convert the users into customers. Whether you are a social media influencer yourself or a brand, if you want to grow your account or brand further, mastering TikTok influencer marketing is a must-known skill for you. Also, if you are a TikTok influencer, you need to understand how your cooperating brands are thinking to get more and better cooperation as well as maximize your profits. There is no better time to develop your TikTok influencer marketing strategy. Even for brands with smaller budgets on marketing, the influencer-led TikTok campaigns provide creative and cost-effective solutions to drive awareness and engagement in a short time.

1. How Brands Execute TikTok Marketing

The TikTok marketing ecosystem is relatively new, while more and more brands are tapping into this platform to advertise. Here are several different ways to do TikTok marketing

1. **Brand takeover ads**

This type of ad can be bought for several brands categories, including food, fitness, fashion, etc. TikTok provides one brand to take over a category every day. The brand takeover ads show as a user opens the TikTok app, which means brands can get immediate attention. These ads aim to prompt users to click on the CTA to visit the brand's landing page, either external or internal to the app. Users are also allowed to tap to skip the ad if they don't want to take action. Brands can expect up to $50,000/day for a brand takeover with 5 million guaranteed impressions.

2. In-feed ads

These in-feed video ads blend nicely with TikTok's feed of the short videos. Three action models can be run here: CPM (cost per impression), CPV (cost per 6-second view), and CPC (cost per click).

TikTok provides targeting based on gender, age, and geo-location. Also, marketers can create custom audiences with the option of blacklisting or whitelisting profiles. It comes with a $6,000 minimum campaign spend at a $10 cost per impression.

3. TikTok shoppable ads: hashtag challenge plus

This TikTok's new shoppable ad format – the hashtag challenge plus refers to when brands sponsor hashtags to create a dedicated experience for users to explore both video content and products. To make this feature altogether more versatile, it takes hashtag challenge ads with a shoppable component.

As users land on the hashtag challenge page, they are able to click on either the Explore tab or the Videos tab. The Videos tab can introduce users to a slew of video content that is tagged with the hashtag prompting users to submit their own tagged content. If users choose to click into the Explore section, they will be led to the shopping experience where the brands show products for users to sift through. Users can click "Shop Now" to visit the brand's website, where they can finish the checkout process.

4. TikTok hashtag challenge ads

This takes the TikTok challenge culture and puts it into the advertisement format. This type of ad promotes branded hashtags to encourage the submission of user-generated content that features their participation in the challenge.

Displaying as a banner on the Discover page, this ad can direct users to a page with instructions on the participation way featuring a feed of other participants' content too. Even though brands can make their own hashtag without purchasing it as an ad, branded hashtag challenge can guarantee more impressions.

5. TikTok influencer marketing ads

It enables brands to partner with TikTok influencers

to make and share sponsored content with their viewers. A number of brands have already experimented with cooperating with TikTok influencers, most with great success. The influencer marketing ads will perform well if TikTok creators are given creative freedom, the content discloses the sponsorship, and the partnership is authentic. TikTok is growing more sophisticated, and the tracking capabilities are going to allow brands to have more direct insights into the TikTok influencer marketing campaign performance.

6. Branded TikTok stickers

This is another way brands can entice TikTok users to engage with their content. For example. The NFL released player AR stickers allowing users to find them in the "football" effects folder in the video creation tool. This ad provides brands with a more interactive experience, which is less intrusive compared to traditional-style ads.

2. Step-by-Step To Launch A TikTok Influencer Campaign

Even though TikTok influencer marketing has just been around a short time, brands are putting the pedal to the medal with the influencer campaigns on TikTok. To develop an impactful marketing strategy, marketers should follow the following steps:

1. Research and Understand TikTok

As you read so far, you should be on your way

to learning whether or not TikTok is a good fit for your brand. You can either test new ways of reaching your target audience or partner with an established TikTok influencer/reputable influencer marketing agency.

2. Decide your TikTok campaign goals

What's your ultimate goal for your brand's campaign? Will it encourage users to download your app or drive UGC? Also, consider the outcomes and determine which KPIs you will use to measure your campaign's success. Your clearly defined goal will allow you to measure your campaign's ROI and the overall strategy.

3. Carefully research and vet TikTok influencers

Do your due diligence about the TikTok creators you would like to partner with.

- o Is their audience in line with yours?
- o Do they already have a proven track record of delivering high-quality content & gaining positive engagement?
- o Do their values and interests authentically match yours?

Avoid partnering with a TikTok influencer based only on vanity metrics (like the likes and followers). Carefully do your research to make sure the influencer is a natural fit.

4. Allow TikTok influencers to express creativity

It can be tempting for you to want to exercise too much control over the content. Learn to trust the creators you found who are native to the platform and the niche. They are also the ones who already have established authenticity in the space and know better what their followers' preferences are.

So avoid taking away their creative spark and let the influencers have their own input. This can also go a long way in developing your long-term relationship.

5. Measure your TikTok campaign results

This goes without saying while executing the marketing campaign without knowing the way to measure its performance is futile. Learn general benchmarks of strong performance so that you are able to test constantly and optimize your influencer marketing strategy on TikTok.

For example, if your goal is brand awareness, check the number of views the collaboration makes and how much engagement the campaign generates. Also, make sure to have link tracking in place with conversion-based campaigns.

6. Make sure TikTok influencer sponsorships are FTC-compliant

You may have worked with other influencers on other social media platforms. Then you probably know that FTC violations can be costly to your brand. So make sure the TikTok influencers use #ad complying with FTC guidelines without getting into a legal mess.

7. Test other TikTok advertising formats

TikTok influencer marketing can be a lucrative endeavor for your brand, so why not pair it with other TikTok advertising methods to get the most of this platform? This can boost your brand's presence and bolster your overall efforts of TikTok marketing.

3. Tips For Finding TikTok Influencers

To begin a TikTok influencer marketing campaign, you should exercise your best judgment to find reputable TikTok influencers to partner with. The influencers you select will represent your brand, and failing to research influencers carefully can put your brand at risk of falling short with the TikTok marketing campaigns. Also, you need to be familiar with what's important to those influencers in a brand partnership.

Here are five tips on finding the right TikTok influencers to prepare your brand's successful TikTok influencer marketing campaign.

1. Know your target users

The first step is to decide if your target users are on TikTok. If they are, understand which influencers can best resonate with them. Never assume TikTok creators with the most followers will be the most impactful. Do your due diligence on which influencers will be able to generate the most meaningful engagement and if they can affect buying decisions.

2. Do an organic Google search

Many times, perform a target Google search will yield helpful results. Begin searching "top TikTok creators" to find some of those more popular TikTokers, then narrow down your search to the particular niche. For instance, if you are a makeup product brand, typing in "fashion TikTok creators" could be a logical starting place. Please note that TikTok is still in its infancy at present, and the lists of top creators can constantly be changing.

3. Search trending and relevant hashtags on the Discover page

One trick about TikTok is that the desktop experience provides a little more navigational control. Looking to search specific user handles, keywords, and hashtags are better off using the mobile app. With that being said, go to the Discover page and type in your search terms in the top search bar. You will be able to identify the top trending videos from the "Hashtags," "Top," "Sounds," "Videos," and "Users" tabs.

4. Find existing influencer sponsored content

You are also able to search for video content tagged with #ad to find sponsored content on TikTok. This approach allows you to locate existing influencer content fast and decide if those influencers will be worth reaching out to for collaboration opportunities.

5. Cross-check the influencers you already knew from other social media platforms

It's always good to check on the influencers you already find from other popular social media platforms, such as YouTube and Instagram. If you already know some influencers from other platforms, you can check how they are doing on TikTok. Influencers of all sizes typically boast a solid cross-channel presence, which means if they are performing well on YouTube and Instagram, they may also have a growing fanbase on TikTok. However, this is not always the case. So it's worth checking in on the influencers you've already worked with or heard of on other platforms.

TikTok Influencer Marketing Platforms

Understandably, if you got exhausted all choices above, it will make sense to leverage TikTok influencer marketing platforms to find and pick the right TikTok influencers. Please note that since TikTok is still an emerging social platform, not every influencer marketing platform has updated its databases to show the TikTok influencers' popularity. Below are several top influencer marketing platforms that you can use as a discovery tool:

1. Fanbytes

It can help you find influencers across multiple social media platforms, and TikTok is their most recent addition. As the first platform dedicated to TikTok, Fanbytes introduces you to over half a million TikTok influencers.

Besides, it can also give you access to the TikTokers' bios and the influences who mentioned other brands before. It also runs its own TikTok influencer campaigns, which makes it a reliable resource for identifying the right influencers on TikTok.

2. Julius

As a leading influencer marketing solution, Julius allows you to filter through a database of over 100,000 influencers that was vetted with the help of human review.

They offer multiple filters for you to narrow down a list of influencers based on several search criteria. Even though TikTok influencers are not searchable on it currently, TikTok itself is using Julius, which means there's a high chance this platform can roll out TikTok search capabilities later.

3. Upfluence

This influencer discovery tool offers a database of over one million influencers and features some of those top TikTok influencers. Upfluence's keyword search function is able to ensure granular results while less precise for TikTokers.

It may not provide you with a very comprehensive list, but you still can identify those who are top TikTok performers and branch out in their network since the majority of them are usually well-connected to other influencers in the same space. For example, if you identify a TikTok influencer A, you can scan through his fans and video content to find other popular creators to who he is connected.

4. What To Consider When Working With TikTok Influencers

After you find the right influencers for your campaign, now it's time to begin working with them. Here are several general rules of thumb for working with any influencer to make sure sponsored content is authentic. These should be reflected clearly in the influencer contract too.

To develop a solid influencer contract, keep the following in mind:

1. Ownership clause

Don't repurpose or reshare influencer-generated content without their permission first. At the beginning of a campaign, you should define the partnership terms and clearly state that you tend to reuse the TikTok influencers' content for marketing purposes. Also, specify the duration of content ownership.

2. Influencer creativity

Refrain from controlling the TikTok influencers' voice and process too much and give them creative freedom. TikTok is built with creatives, so it won't do any good to take that component from a creator away. By stifling TikTok influencers, sponsored content doesn't resonate with their viewers. Just trust what has worked for them and consider them an extension of your business.

3. Specific deliverables

To make sure your TikTok influencer marketing campaign gets smooth, you should communicate what they envision, such as talking points, audio/visual elements, and the formats of these points. This is to help you avoid a catastrophic disconnection between execution and expectations.

4. Brand messaging directives

Let your influencers know your campaign's major goal and the message you want them to convey, which will help eliminate the back-and-forth of some disorganized campaigns without predefined objectives. This will also help prevent influencers from missing the mark with your business's messaging.

5. FTC disclosure

Ask TikTok influencers to disclose the sponsorship clearly, making sure they comply with FTC guidelines. This can be offering the verbiage TikTok influencers need to use, either verbal or written. Use the #ad typically suffices on TikTok.

6. Exclusivity clause

Set a time frame for TikTok influencers that will prohibit them from engaging with your competitors. Imagine if you failed to define these terms and your influencer collaborates with your direct competitor the week after your own partnership. Their content for you will be less trustworthy and impactful.

7. Clear deadlines

To ensure your campaign runs as planned, set deadlines for deliverables. This includes set your campaign's duration, deadlines to deliver content for your approval, as well as the dates and times the influencers must share the sponsored content.

5. How To Generate Positive ROI

Now, it's time for you to consider all the factors determining how well TikTok influencers perform. That is the ROI. Even if TikTok creators are the experts at nurturing engagement, you also should understand how to best integrate your brand's values, voice, or/and product into TikTok influencer content to gain the most actionable engagement. Besides drumming up buzz around your brand, it's also vital that the influencers can drive real results that translate into customers, whether immediately or in the future.

When partnering with TikTok influencers, you should aim to generate:

- **Positive brand sentiment** (such as UGC, brand mentions);
- **High engagement** (including views, likes, and comments);
- **Conversions** (such as signups, purchases, or downloads).

To achieve these goals, TikTok influencers need to ensure sponsored videos hold true to their interests and values. The TikTok sponsored content should be authentic to drive positive ROI.

Failing to deliver authenticity, influencers risk losing their audience's trust, falling short of campaign goals, and subsequently harming the sponsor brand's reputation.

Must-Haves for Driving Positive ROI

To have authentic and meaningful engagement, the content made by TikTok creators needs to drive actional results with their viewers, including resharing, liking, commenting, or submitting UGC in response to the sponsored content.

It also can come in the form of users participating in a branded hashtag challenge, following your brand's TikTok account, mentioning your brand positively, or visiting your website to finish the transaction.

Besides these engagement factors, you should understand how TikTok's algorithm operates to give the sponsored content the best chance of performing successfully.

The following content ideas do exceptionally well:

1. **Trendsetting**: content accentuating a current trend or creating a new trend on TikTok.
2. **Original**: Highly imaginative and creative content captivating the audience in new ways.
3. **Visual & audio effect**: Striking design elements and catch tunes helping boost memorability of your products.
4. **Duets**: Content format in which users can show a split-screen next to another user's video, which can spur higher levels of engagement.
5. **Challenges**: the tagged video that's easily trendy, inclusive, recognizable, searchable, and entices audiences to participate.
6. **Hashtags**: Use hashtags cleverly to spark hashtag trends, engage more users, and increase tagged content's discoverability.
7. **eCommerce**: Influencers are given a promo code to share in their videos, which passes on savings to their viewers. This is a great way to attract new customers.

8. **Before and After:** Testimonials are well-known for impacting purchase decisions heavily. We cannot think of a testimonial more powerful compared to the before and after.

6. TikTok Influencer Marketing Campaigns To Inspire You

- **Levi's**

In order to celebrate the new "shop now" button launch, TikTok collaborated with Levi's on the recent influencer campaign.

Levi's has worked with 4 TikTok influencers in that campaign and personalized their denim with its Future Finish 3D customization technology. Creators' videos were displayed as in-feed ads. TikTok users were encouraged to click on the "Shop Now" button within a specific time frame if they wanted to get the unique designs.

According to Levi's report, the watch time for these influencers' videos was twice as long as the platform average on TikTok.

Also, the views for Levi.com's "Future Finish" product pages got doubled for every product mentioned in the videos.

- **Walmart**

Walmart has executed TikTok influencer marketing campaigns several times. For example, in their #DealDropDance, users were encouraged to share videos of themselves dancing in the Walmart aisles for a chance to win a $100 gift card. They collaborated with TikTok influencers, including former NFL star and actor Terry Crews, comedian Drea Knows Best, singer Montana Tucker, gamer Kidrl, dancer BDash, etc.

Cemeronfromwalmat, who is a young Walmart employee, also participated in this campaign and has become popular on TikTok for his dancing in Walmart.

Additionally, #DealDropDance has won a shorty award and gained over two million impressions. So what has made this campaign so successful? Walmart has chosen a variety of influencers to help increase reach. The fact that participation was very simple - #DealDropDance had just eight simple moves allowing almost everybody could participate.

- **Gymshark**

Gymshart has partnered with 6 TikTok influencers to increase their brand awareness and boost sales. Their campaign is known as **66 Day | Change Your Life Challenge**.

This challenge encouraged TikTok users to set personal goals and post their progress continually under #gymshark66.

One interesting thing is that four out of the six selected TikTok influencers are twins. And each covered a niche – fitness, dance, challenges, comedy, fashion, or beauty. Also, all are from different countries and have millions of fans. As a result, Gymshart was able to reach more than 19.8 million fans and an 11.11% engagement rate. After this campaign, #gymshark66 has earned over 122 million views.

Conclusion

As you plan your TikTok influencer marketing strategy, think about the best and worst-case situations. Don't need to be afraid to show your brand's human side. Also, don't forget that the best influencer campaigns are born out of close collaboration and meaningful relationships.

Every social media platform has its specificities. For sure, TikTok has taken the internet by surprise. It will stay for as long as the public wants to enjoy the quality and straight-on-point entertainment.

Give your business a boost by making it more appealing to young generations. As doing TikTok marketing and other social influencer marketing, try to be as original and creative as possible. Integrate your business within the TikTok videos while avoid creating all the content around your brand.

Section: TikTok Monetization

As TikTok is becoming so popular, one question arose with it quickly: "Can you make money on this thing?" Yes, you definitely can. Although TikTok is not built specifically for monetization and bring income streams to its creators, this platform is super commercial-friendly. Many creators have earned a living by using this platform creatively.

1. How Much You Can Earn On TikTok

TikTok statistics showing it's excellent for monetization

TikTok is the most promising platform for affiliate marketing and content creation. App Annie has forecasted that there are 1.2 billion monthly users on TikTok. Here are some exciting stats that prove its great monetization capabilities:

- **$1 billion creator fund**: TikTok is investing in its top content creators;
- **$54 million**: global user spending in 1.5 years;
- **$5 million**: earned by star 19-year TikToker in 2020;
- **$25-125 per post**: according to Influencer Marketing Hub, this is the estimated earning of a micro-TikTok influencer.

How much can you earn?

If you are thinking of monetizing your TikTok account, you are actually asking yourself: "how much can I make here?" Like other social apps or networks, the answer will not be a detailed 6-figure number. While we are able to speculate with the facts.

Social media experts have estimated that it's likely to get 2 to 3 cents per 1,000 views on TikTok. Let's say you have 300-400k followers, and then you can charge around $350 for every affiliate post. London-based economist Tom Hartmann has published on *Medium*, stating that the TikTok creators with 100,000 followers are able to make around $500 - $2,000 for sponsored posts. If we do the math, that means the top TikTok influencers can make somewhere between $50,000 to $150,000 for a sponsored video.

We can also estimate earnings by reviewing figures published by marketing agencies. For example, TalentX Entertainment estimates they charge brands between $0.01 to $0.02 for every video view on TikTok.

In addition, Influencer Marketing Hub came up with a great tool for better estimating TikTok earnings: TikTok Money Calculator, which allows you to calculate your estimated earnings from your TikTok account.

How much you can earn on TikTok varies, while similar to other social media platforms, it can be very lucrative if your video goes viral. As mentioned, there's TikTok creators' fund. TikTok wants to encourage creators to make content full-time on this platform. They haven't revealed what the full-time income might look like. However, we can see the idea is that it will be substantial enough to make a living on TikTok without having to work other jobs.

2. Top Ways You Can Make Serious Money On TikTok

#1 Grow You TikTok Account & Sell It

This is already hot on Instagram. For example, a 23-year-old Instagram user, Ramy Halloun, has made $30,000 per year from flipping Instagram accounts. This method can be replicated on TikTok.

To begin, find a niche and start making interesting content in that niche. Once you grow your accounts to a certain level of engagement and followers, you can reach out to those brands in that industry and sell your TikTok accounts to them.

The themed accounts are the easiest types of accounts to sell. It'll be more challenging to sell personal accounts since the new owners won't easily replicate them. With a themed profile, you will be able to find buyers easily. The followers of the accounts are engaging with the accounts because of their themes. They may not even notice the ownership change.

For instance, if your TikTok account is about the

videos of popular travel adventures and destinations. You will easily sell the account to any business that provides travel services. Also, you can do similar things for other industries like food, fitness, beauty, fashion, etc.

The important thing is to create an account with high-quality content. The better engagement rate and more followers your TikTok account has, the higher price you can sell it for.

#2 Live Stream

TikTok fans are able to help their favorite creators make money without brands. Even though the actual exchange rates can vary with time, the basic system is straightforward: TikTok users can use actual money to buy "coins" through in-app purchases. Then they can use their coins to tip their favorite TikTok creators as a thank-you for making some good live content.

TikTok will pass 80% of the value of the tip onto the creator. What can the creator do with these coins? They can turn the coins into diamonds that can be converted into cash by PayPal.

Sounds cool, right? It may not sounds like a fortune, but it still can be an income stream.

#3 Live Stream + eCommerce

TikTok is working to build a stronger monetization process to capitalize on its huge potential. One key element of this will be eCommerce. Back in 2019, it has been working on its eCommerce offerings for a while and testing the basic eCommerce links within clips. Bloomberg has reported that TikTok is now developing its live-stream shopping events integrating with Shopify to present product ads in-stream.

With TikTok revealing more new eCommerce choices coming soon to the app, such as "Promo Tiles," you will be able to add promotional alerts, customizable sales, overlaid on the video clips, as well as "Showcase Tiles" that better enable creators to promote products in their uploads directly.

#4 Publish sponsored posts

This is a popular way to make money on TikTok. Based on *Business Insider*, you are able to make an average of $0.01 to $0.02 for every sponsored view on TikTok. For example, if you have a video with 100,000 views, you will make $1000 in sponsorships.

Once you have built a following on TikTok, try to reach out to brands and provide your services. Don't forget the best part is that you won't need to have millions of followers before you can pitch to brands. If you have a few thousands of engaged followers, you are good to go.

Do your research and look for brands that are

interested in building their presence on TikTok, and then reach out to them. At the same time, analyze the influencers in your industry to see those sponsors they work with, which will give you a better idea of brands to reach out to.

After you get your list of target sponsors, send them a brief by emailing them. The following are the things you need to include in your pitch:

- Who you are;
- What you are doing;
- What makes you an expert in your niche or industry;
- Vital metrics, including engagement rate and follower count;
- What you have achieved. You could share success stories from your previous sponsored campaigns.

Pro tip: as you are just beginning, it's smart to work with those smaller brands first, which can help you build your portfolio more efficiently.

#5 Promoting & Selling Your Own Merchandise

This is probably the most practical way for most creators to earn some money on TikTok. The best part is that you won't need thousands of followers or become a national-scale influencer before selling your own services and products.

The secret is having some other lines of stores or business, and you can use TikTok as a free way to promote and sell your services or products. You can also promote your existing business for sure. Another great thing is that your business can be any legal services or business, whether crafty, nerdy, techy or even a little bit crazy.

For instance, you might have a business selling beauty products. Then you can make creative 15-second makeup tutorial videos and post them on TikTok. Add your promotional advertising your own products and the way customers can reach you in the last 3 seconds of your videos.

By doing this, even though TikTok won't directly paying you for anything, your business is making thousands of dollars on new customers you are attracting with your videos. (Don't forget to put the videos on your YouTube Channel or Facebook Page if you have.)

#6 Affiliate Marketing

Compared to getting sponsored for your posts, one advantage of affiliate marketing is that you are able to earn money from promoting affiliate products or services even without the need to reach those brands directly.

Brands need to expose their services and products. They typically decide what they are willing to pay for: an order, a purchase, installing an app, and more. These are known as conversions.

To do affiliate marketing, you'll need to register on an affiliate network and select the offers you are willing to promote. Every offer has a unique referral link signaling to an advertiser every time a customer completes the action.

You will get paid every time someone uses your link and completes the required action (placing an order, signing up for the course, installing an app, or downloading a trial version.)

Popular affiliate markets include:

- Digistore24.com
- Clickbank.com
- JvZoo
- Cj.com
- Shareasale.com

#7 Amazon Referral Links

This is another type of affiliate marketing. We introduce it as a separate method here is because, unlike other affiliate marketplaces, Amazon usually has a higher standard of choosing their affiliate marketers and requires your application. If you don't do it right, it could end up costing you your Amazon account since they prohibit any linked system that spoofs and obscures them from being capable of telling where a given link came from.

To do this right, use your bio as the primary place where you can write information on TikTok. Yes, your bio can include text, but it won't be clickable. So what can you do?

We've introduced several ways in the previous section. Here is another way: focus your bio on one short text string, that is, a shortened URL to your affiliate marketing landing page to make the link sweeter. Then on your affiliate marketing landing page, put your actual Amazon referral links. Don't forget to make sure you have the right affiliate links for your viewers. For example, if you've done a 15-second lipsync of a Justin Bieber song. It probably won't inspire anyone to order the basketball equipment from Amazon from your landing page. Instead, try to inspire them to buy Justin's album directly.

Amazon Influencer Program

This program welcomes you by promising an exclusive URL on Amazon's products. You then can use it to recommend the products to your followers. This is an excellent opportunity if your following is massive enough.

#8 Manage Influencer Campaigns

There are straight-up influencer agencies to serve Instagram influencers already. We can apply this concept to TikTok. You can be the broker or middleman between TikTok influencers and a brand that wants to work with them.

You can charge a service fee by managing both parties, creating the agreements, ensuring the deliverables are all met, and managing influencer campaigns.

TikTok is smart too. Actually, they already have a built-in internal influencer program. Brands will need to pay a percentage to TikTok for brokering the agreement, and it can be expensive. Smaller brands usually will probably prefer to work with influencer agencies to save money.

As an influencer agency, you can help brands strategize, execute, and manage TikTok influencer campaigns. You also will help brands decide the best influencers to work with. Also, you can take it a step further by creating a social marketing strategy in order to meet the brands' goals.

The followings are what you should be able to do if you want to run an influencer agency:

- Identify high-performing influencers with a good track record;

- Develop a relationship with top TikTok influencers;

- Run successful influencer and social media marketing campaigns;

- Create successful influencer campaigns for various advertising categories, which can help you diversify your income stream.

It does take time and effort to start a reputable influencer agency. It's crucial that you begin your agency right away to get ahead of the curve. The best part is that you don't need to limit your services to just TikTok. You also will be able to run influencer campaigns for other social media platforms.

#9 Management Services

You also can make money by providing management services for TikTok creators. Many creators have millions of followers, and this can happen really fast, even overnight for some of them. When this happens, it's like having a business land in their lap.

This is where you can step in and provide services to help them with their content strategy, manage offers and deals coming their way.

If you are good at storytelling, you can definitely apply that to providing management services to TikTok influencers.

#10 TikTok's Creator Fund

As mentioned a little bit earlier, TikTok has introduced their Creator Fund, supporting creators to monetize from the app directly. It's to encourage creators who dream of using their creativity and voices to spark inspirational careers.

What we have known is that the US fund started with $200 million to support TikTok creators, and funds are being distributed over the upcoming year and will continue growing. To be eligible, you must be:

- At least 18 years old;
- Having more than 100k followers;
- Having 100,000 authentic video views in the last 30 days;
- Consistently posting original content following TikTok's guidelines.

TikTok's creator fund is their latest response to their commitment to their creators. They also outline the following financial opportunities for creators:

- $50 million Creative Learning Fun, introducing emerging teachers to the platform. This benefitted more than 1,000 US TikTokers who've been affected by the Covid-19 pandemic.

- To help brands identify and collaborate with innovative creators to partner on paid campaigns, TikTok develops their Creator Marketplace to drive awareness and attract new customers.

These resources significantly impact TikTok creators, allowing them to continue doing what they love and financially empowering them to make positive impacts. The Creator Fund is considered a major step for TikTok to become a reliable income source for TikTok rising stars and their families.

TikTok pays creators and entices them to post more frequently, keeping fans interested and engaged and ultimately growing the platform.

#11 Consulting

Once you become a TikTok pro, and you already understand how someone can take a video that may get a hundred views and help them earn thousands of views, you can go ahead and provide consulting services.

This is an amazing way to leverage your expertise from TikTok and help people who want to be popular TikTok influencers boost their strategy.

Of course, you should have the background and the experience first to provide this service. However, once you are there, other people will be willing to pay to have your expertise and experience on their accounts.

If you can help them get influencer agreements or any deals, you can even negotiate a percentage as their consultant.

If you are a TikTok expert, there are tons of brands and even individuals that will pay you for your services.

So, if you know how to get thousands, even millions of views on your TikTok videos, why not teach others how to do the same for a consulting fee? This is not a fantastic way to leverage your expertise but also diversify your income.

Sean Young is a good example of a TikTok consultant. He is able to make $10,000 per month advising celebrities and businesses on the best type of content for their brands. You can see that there's money to be made here. So, if you do understand the platform and have a track record for making viral TikTok videos with high engagement rates, try to begin teaching others how to do so to build another income stream.

3. Making Money on TikTok Vs. YouTube Vs. Instagram

Youtube also pays creators based on advertising dollars made from creating videos for this platform. However, TikTok doesn't have a specific equation for how their creators are paid, which is more like Instagram.

The following table shows the difference between the three platforms:

	TikTok	Instagram	YouTube
Active Monthly Users (Globally)	Around 700 million	Over 1 billion	Over 2 billion
Monetization Ways	-Host a Livestream -Brand partnerships -Product sales -TikTok Creator's Fund	-Brand partnerships -Product sales	-Channel memberships -Brand partnerships -Ad money from YouTube -Product sales
Entry Barriers	-Need a smartphone -Need relationships with brands	-Need a smartphone -Could need photo editing or graphic design knowledge to succeed -Need relationships with brands	-Need a smartphone -Might need audio or lighting equipment

Section: Best TikTok Tools To Triple Your TikTok Account Growth

It does take time and effort to grow your TikTok account, and it can be challenging to stand out from the crowd. Fortunately, there are tools that not only can help you make this process easier but also help you manage your TikTok presence, whether you are a regular user, an influencer, or a brand. After analyzing the behaviors and growth analytics of TikTok influencers, we've picked the best TikTok tools on the market for your ultimate success without burning out in a TikTok vortex.

For better channelization among each space, we've divided these tools into three major sub-parts:

Part #1 Best TikTok Tools for Video Editing

1. TikTok Built-in Video Editor

You are able to jump to TikTok's interesting inbuilt edition section once you finish recording your video. Its built-in video editor can help you do the basic tasks, including adding soundtracks, filters, blurring, etc. To present both the recording and editing interface, tap on the "+" icon. Tapping on **Add a sound** will let you go through TikTok's huge media library.

Key Features

- Several options are available in **Filters, Beauty, Speed, Flip, Timer**, etc.
- **Flip** is a feature helping switch the camera mode.
- **Beauty** mode allows for shadow removal and smoothness.
- **Mixer** is for adjusting the playback sound levels.
- **Trim** can let you shorten the video length.
- **Playback speed** is able to be changed from slow motion to fast motion (for example, 0.1x to 3x)

2. Viamaker

This is a free and all-in-one video editing app to help you make appealing TikTok videos. Viamaker is a new app from the TikTok creator- Bytedance. They play together nicely. It's also easy to use. You will be able to **reverse, trim, and add speed change effects** to your TikTok videos. You also can add a personal and creative touch by using its **advanced filters**. In addition, it includes a massive **music library** for you to engage visitors with fun sounds. Don't forget to express yourself with those custom TikTok fonts and trending stickers.

3. Wondershare Filmora9 Video Editor

Plenty of influencers use external video editors to make their videos stand out. Whether your videos are about music, travel, business, game, vlog, education, or family, WondershareFilmora 9 is here to help with advanced and easy-to-use editing solutions.

Key Features

- It provides a range of beautiful filters and overlays for amazing editing.
- Its Filmstock has loads of royalty-free video files, audio files, stock images, video effects, etc., which is a handy tool for TikTok content creators.
- The Video Editing Academy can help you learn photography and editing skills.
- Its 24/7 user-friendly support provides you tips on growth and other support channels.

Part #2 Best TikTok Tools for Marketing

1. TokUpgrade

TokUpgrade is one of the first TikTok growth services providing comprehensive managed services. It stands out among other similar platforms because of its intricate working TikTok knowledge, which all their account managers have put into their daily users' strategies.

After you sign up to TokUpgrade, your own dedicated account manager will contact you and help you set up your service. So before you sign up, it's worth thinking about who your target audience is as your account manager will ask you detailed questions about this.

From there, they will start growing your TikTok

account. Unlike other services that just focus on one avenue, TokUpgrade's multipronged strategy will ensure your account's maximum growth. They use hashtags, follow/unfollow methodology, engagement, and locations. All these work together to make a cohesive organic growth strategy, helping you grow your account at a sustainable rate.

Besides, you don't need to worry about putting your account at risk since they have been aware of the limits imposed by TikTok. So they won't put daily actions over TikTok, which results in a secure and safe platform for you to use.

2. TokSocial

TokSocial offers its users a useable and well-designed interface allowing you to track your growth and whether your strategies are working.

Similar to TokUpgrade, your account manager will contact you and begin helping you develop your strategy once you sign up. What makes it an effective TikTok growth companion is its understanding of TikTok's algorithm and how to work with it instead of against it. TokSocial's ability to work with the algorithm will prevent your TikTok account from getting removed or banned for deploying a growth service.

One advantage that TokSocial has is the advanced targeting that is really able to help you narrow down your target demographic and market and grow your audience. If you notice an area that wasn't performing as expected, you can change who you are targeting and related data within this platform to develop a new strategy.

Buying TikTok followers may look attractive, but this is a short-term move that won't necessarily add much value to your account if you do want to engage with a genuine audience. However, when you use TokSocial to help you grow your TikTok account, you are making sure that your follower-to-engagement ratio is well-maintained and the users that begin following you are genuine ones who will enjoy seeing your content.

3. Task Ant

If you prefer a more analytical approach, Task Ant is for you. It uses a mixture of easy, medium, and hard-rank hashtags to help you increase your reach on TikTok. They have built a complex score indicator allowing you to identify different hashtag types easily. For example, if you search for travel hashtags, you just view the top trending travel hashtags and check the upload count, average likes as well as the estimated reach for the travel hashtags.

It's also easy to get started and a great tool to use TikTok bots or other growth services since you can simply use hashtag sets you create to give you an added boost of exposure.

4. Loomly

As you are trying to build your social media empire, the last thing you want to do is sit around all day and wait for the best time to post to TikTok. Then Loomly comes in.

It's a social media posting and scheduling tool, helping you publish, collaborate, and measure your social media marketing efforts from just one platform. It provides a content library, optimization tips, post ideas, and more.

If you work with a team, Loomly can notify you every time your team member comments on or updates a piece of content via Slack, email, and Microsoft Teams notifications.

Their scheduling tool is one of our favorites. You will be able to schedule your TikTok posts, and you will know when it's time to publish with Loomly's help.

Key Features:

- Get post ideas based on RSS feeds, date-related events, trending topics, and social media best practices.

- List and calendar views to keep your social media content calendar organized.

- Content with your team for an approved workflow, a collaborative review, with end-to-end post and ad history.

- Organize, store, and use your notes, videos, links, photos, and post templates in an intuitive, central library.

5. SocialPilot

It's a cost-effective and simple social media marketing tool for teams and agencies. Over 115,000 businesses use SocialPilot to manage their scheduled posts, analyze results, and improve engagement.

SocialPilot allows you to make and schedule multiple TikTok videos to expand your reach so you can make sure your content will get seen and your posting strategy keeps on track.

It's especially helpful to manage multiple accounts. You are capable of scheduling videos for multiple accounts seamlessly by setting up individual posting schedules.

Key Features:

- URL shortening keeps your URLs looking as appealing as your videos.

- Content curation helps you identify relevant and trending content for various keywords and influencers.

- Schedule and share content from anywhere over the internet

6. Analisa.io

This is another great tool for profile and hashtag analysis. You are able to peep through any influencer's profile. Analyzing influencers is vital for marketing, whether you are influencers, media publishers, and brand marketers.

Key Features:

- It helps in competitive analysis, overall profile analysis, campaign reporting, influencer mapping, follower demographics, and authenticity checks.

- It breaks down the analysis of rates into comment rate, likes rate, and engagement rate.

- It's an AI-powered platform to get insights for hashtags, followers, and public profiles.

- It shows posting maps if geotagged, together with posting activity and audience engagement.

7. Pentos

This tool can help you make your TikTok analysis very easy. It offers you overall performance and review of other TikTok accounts. It can be hard to analyze other TikTok profiles with the current API. This tool can help with corrective analysis.

Also, you will get needed insights on trending challenges on the TikTok platform.

Key Feature:

- It offers an in-depth analysis of the TikTok profile, including views, hearts, comments, engagement rates, etc.

- The discovery of detailed data gets checked regarding songs, hashtags, public profiles, and other posts.

Part #3 Best TikTok Tools to Gain More Following

1. Media Mister

Whether you just started your TikTok account or want to boost your followers' numbers fast, Media Mister can offer the solution. It provides high-quality followers that can be instantly put onto their TikTok account. Since they already have been operating across various platforms for a long time, they know what followers will be best for every account.

Its ability to purchase followers and likes makes Media Mister stand out from its competitors. As mentioned, the follower-to-engagement ratio is vital. So it's better to purchase followers and likes together. Surely, you can only buy likes without followers to push up your engagement rate. However, if you look to grow your account exponentially, purchase both at a relatively even level to make sure the best follower-to-engagement ratio.

You can also choose a set time frame to distribute your likes or followers. Not only will this ensure that your account maintains the same amount of actions each day, but also it won't flag any of

TikTok's algorithms to your activity, preventing your account from being deleted or disabled.

They guarantee both value for quality and money, which makes it a pretty top-notch company.

2. FollowersUp

FollowersUp offers users who want their accounts to grow fast with an amazing comprehensive service comprising fans, likes, views, comments, shares, auto views, and auto likes. All these factors will work together to give your TikTok account maximum visibility and reach.

Similar to Media Mister, the more services you buy from them, the longer it's going to have them delivered to your account. Even though some people can see this as problematic, it is a way of keeping your account secure and safe.

It's ideal for TikTokers looking to grow their accounts fast and won't be bothered about having a targeted following. This means if you look for a targeted following, it may not be your best choice for your account since you will not be guaranteed to reach the audience you want to target.

3. TokCaptain

TokCaptain has tried to make buying followers or likes almost seamless. Just with a few clicks, you will add up to 5,000 followers or likes per transaction to whichever post or account you selected.

They provide both standard and premium packages for the likes and followers. It does seem that this part of the TokCaptain strategy needs some more work and streamlining to give us tangible differences within the packages. While since they are a relatively new service, it's understandable that this will need more refining.

Also, when it comes to buying followers, it's better to buy the associate likes to ensure that your followers-to-engagement ratio won't be damaged.

4. Try Jeffrey

TryJeffrey is all about increasing your TikTok growth. Like other companies on this list, they also can help you grow your account quickly. It enables you to connect with dozens of new TikTok followers per day.

What makes them a great choice is that they like to get super specific regarding their engagement growth for you. They will ask you about your niche and target audience and exactly what kind of fans you want to check out your content on TikTok.

In this way, they can ensure that they will only engage with people who are probably interested. Also, they will provide consistent reports about their progress on your behalf, which makes them an excellent option if you prefer to stay in the loop and see where your growth is happening.

5. VIRE

VIRE aims to be the #1 agency to help you grow your fan base, gain more engagement, and be famous on TikTok.

It's able to attract your targeted audience by identifying them through the hashtags you add to VIRE. Their queuing system will make sure these actions are performed safely, which avoids abusing the TikTok service, and your account won't get banned.

In addition, their team will optionally comment, like photos, follow and unfollow other TikTokers on your behalf that they found valuable for your account.

They state that they are not using auto follows, likes, or comments. By applying real interactions, the hope is that your account will receive real interaction back. Your dedicated account manager is going to be the one behind all of your interactions on your account, managing your growth as you continue creating content. There is probably still a limit to how much human-level interaction you can achieve as you measure it against automation.

They state that they play nice with TikTok limits without abusing the service. Besides, they also fight spam and have reported lots of spam profiles and photos to make your account safe with them.

Conclusion

These are all you need to create killer content,

analyze your performance, and boost your TikTok account. However, when using these TikTok tools, remember to shoot videos with ideal equipment so that your editing stands out better than your competitors. Don't forget that TikTok, like other social media platforms, is a great marketing platform if you use it correctly. Therefore, everything needs practice and the use of suitable tools to achieve a goal.

Section: Protect Your TikTok Account

When you follow your trend, cybercriminals are following the trends too. They treat the hype around TikTok as a chance to extend their reach. Con artists, spammers, haters, and malware distributors can weaponize hacked accounts in just a snap. The last thing you want to see is that the account you have spent so much time, energy, and even money to build cannot be accessed one day. So, it's every user's interest to protect their accounts.

In this section, you will learn how to harden the defenses and make your account a hard nut to crack. While before we delve into the protection facet of the matter, let's understand what security concerns about this platform have been unearthed to date.

1. TikTok Security Loopholes

In Jan. 2020, the cybersecurity company Check Point Research experts identified a series of TikTok vulnerabilities that may undermine an account's protection. Based on the white hats, a hypothetical attacker is able to take advantage of these flaws to do the following:

- Upload new videos;
- Erase videos;

- Compromise an account and change the content;
- Change the videos' status of private to public;
- Get the victim's email address and other sensitive information about your account.

One malicious technique is SMS link spoofing. Malware distribution and scams are two common use cases of this technique. A sketchy site will be created as a credential phishing page.

Offensive mechanisms, including cross-site scripting (XSS) or cross-site request forgery (CSRF), can also kick in to execute malicious JavaScript code surreptitiously. This type of abuse can entail disruptive outcomes, which makes it easy for an adversary to tamper with the victim's browser cookies and complete various actions in their name.

The following are the red flags indicating your account is compromised, and you should take immediate actions:

- Your TikTok security email address, password, or phone number tied to your account has been changed;
- Someone is adding or removing videos behind your back;
- Messages are being sent without your permission;
- Your nickname or username has been modified.

2. How To Find Out If Someone Is Using Your TikTok Account

Imagine you logged in from others' devices and forget to log out. You may worry that your account may have been hacked. Actually, it's easy to see whether someone else is using your account:

- Tap Manage devices to check which phones your TikTok account was opened on.
- Tap the trashcan icon next to the relevant gadget and select **Remove** to log out devices that you are not using.
- Change your account passport.

3. TikTok Account Security Tips

The following summarizes what you can do to keep perpetrators from gaining authorized access to your account.

1. Use a strong password

This recommendation may sound vanilla, while it's the stronghold of your account's intactness. Besides making your password at least 12 characters long, include uppercase letters, special characters, and numerals.

At the same time, ensure it looks as random as possible to prevent crooks from guessing your password based on your personal details available on other publicly accessible resources, like social networks.

2. Prevent your password from being automatically saved

Yes, password saving is a handy choice, and TikTok does this by default. However, the whole convenience can be overshadowed by the underlying security risks.

So consider turning the auto password save **OFF** on the side of caution:

- Tap **Settings and privacy**;
- Head to **Security and login**;
- Then slide the **save login info** goggle to the left, which means turning it OFF.

3. Refrain from reusing passwords

Since data breaches do happen, you don't want your authentication info for another account to match the TikTok password. It's a classic instance of potential SPOF (Single Point of Failure) to use the same password across different platforms.

4. Two-factor authentication

Most social networks have a two-factor authentication feature. Instagram, Twitter, and Facebook all support this, and you are able to download an authentication app from Google Play Store or App Store. Personally, I would recommend Google authenticator. With the help of two-factor authentication, if someone discovers your password, they won't be able to access your profile without the one-time codes generated from the app.

5. Log in with verification

When you enable the verification by adding the phone number to account details, TikTok can create a one-time password each time you sign in. Compared to the better-known 2FA (two-factor authentication), the phone technique replaces password protection instead of boosting its efficiency.

6. Stay away from sketchy links

Those cybercriminals often try to social-engineer you into tapping a hyperlink that will lead you to a malicious website hosting a harmful payload. Those links can arrive by malicious redirects caused by malware, phishing emails sent by strangers, or booby-trapped text messages.

As one of the abuse approaches states – the messages can impersonate TikTok too. So don't be gullible and ignore these.

7. Think about what you share

Avoid spilling any PII (personally identifiable information), including the phone number or email address in the video descriptions. Those seasoned hackers can mishandle the information to compromise your profile.

4. How To Get Rid Of Hate & Spam In Comments

Not all users mean well, unfortunately. Some are

there to shower others with insults or ads.

If you want to keep your comments section from becoming a sewer, you can set some restrictions. TikTok allows you to disable comments under a specific video. To do this, open the video, tap the three dots and choose the **Privacy setting**. Tap **Turn off** comments for this video on the setting page.

As influencers, you may want viewers to be able to speak their minds about your videos, but you don't want to remove hate and spam manually in the comments, try using a keyword filter:

- Tap Comment filters;
- There is a TikTok's automatic moderator. Enable Filter spam and offensive comments;
- Turn on Filter keywords and specify the specific words and phrases you don't want to see under your video. TikTok's robot will hide comments containing those keywords.

5. How To Prevent Video Theft In TikTok

One TikTok feature is enabling you to download other people's videos. On one side, it's a convenient way to save the videos you like. On the other side, sneaky TikTokers can steal your mega clips and post them as their own, for example, YouTube. You can disable this option to make it considerably more difficult to steal your videos. To do this, go to settings and choose **OFF** for **Allow download**.

6. How To Remove Spam From Private Messages In TikTok

When your private messages are open to everyone, it means anyone can flood your TikTok account with ads or invitations to follow them. In order to get rid of annoying spam, you can block all incoming messages or only allow your friends to send messages to you. Go to **Who can send you messages**, and choose **Off** or **Friends**.

7.How To Block Annoying Notifications In TikTok

TikTok also lives for your attention. It can keep you apprised of everything little thing happening: new videos, recommendations, comments. And likes. If you get annoyed by endless notifications, turn off those you don't want in your account settings.

- Go to **Settings and privacy**;
- Choose **Push notifications** under **content & activity**;
- Deselect the events that you don't want to be notified about.

8.How To Block Specific Users In TikTok

When some fellow TikTokers get on your nerves, and you don't want them to comment on or even see your videos, you can choose to block them. In order to do this:

- Open their profiles;
- Tap the three-dot icon in the upper right corner
- Choose **Block**;
- Tap **Confirm**.

9.What To Do If Your TikTok Account Got Hacked?

As you spot the slightest sign of a hack attack, immediately go ahead and change your account password. Here is how you can do it: Choose **Settings and privacy**, tap **Manage my account**, and follow the on-screen prompts to finish the procedure. Also, make sure to check the accuracy of your account information.

If you have issues with this, go to the Report a problem under Support. Then you can tap the paper sheet icon in the top right to submit a support ticket describing your detailed situation.

All in all, TikTok is an excellent service bringing lots of bells and whistles to your fingertips and enabling you to express yourself through awesome videos.

Although it's not perfect regarding security, do

your homework and tweak the settings to prevent your previous account from being low-hanging fruit for cyberattacks.

Stay safe.

Conclusion

TikTok has become one of the most widely used social media platforms all over the world. At the time of writing, there are more than 800 million active users with over a billion times downloads. These numbers also seem to be growing rapidly every day.

Based on Iconosquare's reports, people are spending significantly more time on TikTok compared to other social media platforms. TikTok users spend 52 mins per day on TikTok every day.

If your target audience is the younger consumer, you definitely want to give TikTok a closer look. Even though the biggest TikTok demographic age group is still 10 to 20 years, don't forget all ages on this app. Even if you are not targeting younger generations, it's worth at least familiarizing yourself with this platform and taking cues from their playful approach. In addition, as the current 16 to 24 years olds get older, they are very likely to become your target audience. Understanding how they like to engage on social media will be helpful for your business. No matter what platform they are focusing on, you will be better connect with them by familiarizing yourself with TikTok.

The recent popularity of TikTok makes many influencers jump from other social media platforms to it, which gives it an edge as they bring their followers from other platforms.

Let's be honest, the algorithms on Twitter, Instagram, and Facebook are not designed to give you exposure. It's lucky for you to have a small percentage of your audience ever see your posts, and the shelf life of content on those platforms is mere hours. However, on TikTok, this is totally different. TikTok already publicly states that your content has a shelf life of 90 days. You are able to have videos on their For You Page that are months old and still get engagement, followers, and comments from them.

Also, the number of TikTok accounts is growing by the day, which means more competition. In order to stand out from all your competitors, take most of this platform, and potentially gain more profits from TikTok, you need to learn how it works and these strategies. In this book, we have discussed TikTok's most important features, how to choose your own profitable niche, effectively set up your account, make your content go viral, gain more followers, as well as marketing strategies and monetization methods. Also, don't forget to protect your account and your private information on TikTok to stay safe.

TikTok is one of the fastest-growing social networks with many potentials for you to make money online. With the right idea and right approaches, you can become the next TikTok star!

If you are a business owner, take advantage of TikTok to grow your business and bring it to the next level!

Now, it's time for you to take action and start your journey towards your goal!

From the Authors

First, thank you for purchasing this book ***TikTok Marketing with TikTok SEO & Algorithm: Ultimate Money Guide***. We know you could have spent your time reading another book, but you have picked this book for which we are very grateful.

I hope this book added some value to your daily life. If so, it would be super nice if you could share this book with your family and friends by sharing it on _Twitter_ and _Facebook_.

If you enjoyed reading this book and found some benefits from reading it, we would like to hear from you. We want you to know that your feedback and support are extremely important to us. We will appreciate it if you could take some time to **post a review** on Amazon kindly.

You can go to amazon.com/ryp to submit your review. Thank you!

We wish you all the best in your future success!

References

1. *Is TikTok the fastest growing social media platform in 2021?* (2021, June 18). W3 Lab. https://w3-lab.com/is-tiktok-the-fastest-growing-social-media-platform-in-2021/#howdoestiktokinfluencermarketingwork

2. Kornilova, V. (2020, January 9). *Developing Apps Like TikTok: The Step-by-step Guide for 2021.* The APP Solutions. https://theappsolutions.com/blog/development/app-like-tiktok/#contents_1

3. Geyser, W. (2020, August 3). *16 TikTok Hidden Features and TikTok Hacks to Explode Your TikTok Game.* Influencer Marketing Hub. https://influencermarketinghub.com/tiktok-hidden-features/

4. Johnson, T. (2021, July 2). *What is TikTok Live Stream Shopping?* Tinuiti. https://tinuiti.com/blog/paid-social/tiktok-live-stream-shopping/

5. J. (2021, April 13). *New TikTok Creators Features You'll Love In Spring 2021.* MagicLinks Blog. https://www.magiclinks.com/blog/tiktok-creators-features-spring-21/

6. Hutchinson, A., & Hutchinson, A. (2021, June 21). *TikTok Launches "Jumps" Feature to Promote Third-Party Apps and Experiences Within TikTok Clips.* Social Media Today. https://www.socialmediatoday.com/news/tiktok-launches-jumps-feature-to-promote-third-party-apps-and-experiences/602161/

7. Clark, M. (2021, June 21). *TikTok will let creators add mini apps to videos.* The Verge.

https://www.theverge.com/2021/6/21/225439
35/tiktok-jumps-video-apps-recipes-expanded-
functionality-rollout

8. *Niche Trends: How To Find Trending Niches (+10
    examples)*. (2021, May 17). The Niche Guru.
    https://thenicheguru.com/niche-
    research/niche-trends/

9. *What is a niche market?* (2021, May 17). The
    Niche Guru. https://thenicheguru.com/niche-
    research/what-is-a-niche-market/

10. *Niche Competitors Analysis: Leveraging Your
    Competitor's Best Strategies*. (2021, May 20).
    The Niche Guru.
    https://thenicheguru.com/niche-
    research/niche-competitors/

11. Johnston M. (2021, May 19). *How to find your
    niche on TikTok and perfect your content*. Vamp.
    https://vamp-
    brands.com/blog/2020/07/09/how-to-find-
    your-niche-on-tiktok/?lang=zh-hans

12. Sigler, S. (2021, July 18). *The 10 Best TikTok
    Niches To Grow faster (And make money.)*. The
    Niche Guru. https://thenicheguru.com/niche-
    investigation/best-tiktok-niches/

13. Aguiar, R. (2020, October 12). *How To Optimize
    Your TikTok Bio 5 Easy Steps [+ Examples]*.
    Hubspot.
    https://blog.hubspot.com/marketing/optimize-
    tiktok-bio

14. Sher, F. (2020, August 3). *How To Setup Your
    TikTok Profile For Getting More Followers*. Falak
    Digital. https://falakdigital.com/how-to-set-up-
    your-tiktok-profile/

15. Singh, P. (2020, September 3). *6 Killer Ways to Optimize Your Tik Tok Profile in 2020.* Ecommshala. https://ecommshala.com/6-killer-ways-to-optimize-tik-tok-profile-in-2020/
16. S. (2021b, July 22). *10 Best Tips To Create Viral TikTok Videos In 2021.* Bel Around The World. https://www.belaroundtheworld.com/best-tips-to-create-viral-tiktok-videos/
17. *How to Go Viral on TikTok.* (n.d.). Voyageandventure. https://www.voyageandventure.com/how-to-go-viral-on-tiktok/
18. Sharma, P. (2021, June 11). *How to go viral on TikTok in just 5 steps!* Platform to Showcase Innovative Startups and Tech News. https://www.techpluto.com/how-to-go-viral-on-tiktok/#Conclusion
19. *10 Steps to Go Viral on Tik Tok.* (n.d.). The Teen Magazine. Retrieved July 24, 2021, from https://www.theteenmagazine.com/10-steps-to-go-viral-on-tik-tok
20. S. (2021b, February 10). *The 3 Most Effective Hacks On How To Go Viral On TikTok In 2021.* Fanbytes. https://fanbytes.co.uk/how-you-can-go-viral-on-tiktok/
21. Worb, J. (2020, May 15). *How to Find the Best TikTok Hashtags For Your Videos.* Later Blog. https://later.com/blog/tiktok-hashtags/#right
22. K. (2021b, July 22). *The Tiktok Hashtags That Will Get You On FYP Page.* Whimsy Soul. https://whimsysoul.com/the-tiktok-hashtags-that-will-get-you-on-fyp-page/
23. M. (2021c, July 7). *When Is the Best Time to Publish Videos on TikTok?* Boosted.

https://boosted.lightricks.com/when-is-the-best-time-to-publish-videos-on-tiktok/

24. Troncoso, D. J. (2021, June 11). *13 Ways To Increase Your TikTok Followers In 2021.* MarketTap. https://www.markettap.com/tiktok-followers/

25. Ganta, M. (2021, June 20). *Powerful Tips to Boost Your TikTok Followers in 2021.* Socialinsider Blog: Social Media Marketing Insights and Industry Tips. https://www.socialinsider.io/blog/increase-tiktok-followers/#targetaudience

26. KELLY, K. (2021, March 21). *How to Grow Your TikTok Account: 11 Tips.* Socialmediaexaminer. https://www.socialmediaexaminer.com/how-to-grow-your-tiktok-account-11-tips/

27. Lapelosová, K. (2020, May 13). *How to Get More Followers on TikTok.* Later Blog. https://later.com/blog/get-followers-on-tiktok/

28. Cox, S. (2021, June 24). *Growing TikTok Followers: How to Get Free Followers on TikTok [10 Ways].* Filmora. https://filmora.wondershare.com/tiktok/get-free-followers-tiktok-tips.html

29. Santora, J. (2021, April 14). *How to Grow Your TikTok Followers in 2021.* Influencer Marketing Hub. https://influencermarketinghub.com/tiktok-followers/

30. K. (2021b, July 22). *How I Got 10k TikTok Followers Overnight: 9 Hacks To Rapidly Grow Your Following On TikTok.* Whimsy Soul. https://whimsysoul.com/how-i-got-10k-tiktok-

followers-overnight-8-hacks-to-rapidly-grow-your-following-on-tiktok/

31. Mullery, S. (2021, April 12). *How the TikTok Algorithm Works in 2021*. Tinuiti. https://tinuiti.com/blog/paid-social/tiktok-algorithm/

32. Booster Agency. (2020, July 9). *tiktok algorithm metrics Archives*. Booster. https://wearebooster.com/tag/tiktok-algorithm-metrics/

33. Memon, M. (2020, July 29). *How the TikTok Algorithm Works in 2020 (and How to Work With It)*. Social Media Marketing & Management Dashboard. https://blog.hootsuite.com/tiktok-algorithm/

34. T. (2020, November 5). *How TikTok recommends videos #ForYou*. Newsroom | TikTok. https://newsroom.tiktok.com/en-us/how-tiktok-recommends-videos-for-you/

35. Ganta, M. (2021b, June 20). *TikTok Metrics You Should Be Tracking In 2021*. Socialinsider Blog: Social Media Marketing Insights and Industry Tips. https://www.socialinsider.io/blog/tiktok-metrics/#analytics

36. Polner, E. (2021, April 28). *A Guide to TikTok Marketing for Brands: 7 TikTok Metrics You Should Be Tracking*. Octoly - Blog. https://blog.octoly.com/a-guide-to-tiktok-marketing-for-brands-7-tiktok-metrics-you-should-be-tracking/

37. McGlew, M. (2021, June 3). *TikTok Analytics: Your Guide to Understanding the Metrics*. Later Blog. https://later.com/blog/tiktok-analytics/

38. Sehl, K. (2020, August 17). *The Complete Guide to TikTok Analytics: How to Measure Your Success*. Social Media Marketing & Management Dashboard. https://blog.hootsuite.com/tiktok-analytics/

39. mediakix. (2021, March 23). *TikTok Influencer Marketing: How to Work With TikTok Influencers*. https://mediakix.com/influencer-marketing-resources/tik-tok-influencer-marketing/

40. S. (n.d.). *TikTok Influencer Marketing Campaign Examples and Ideas*. Statusphere. Retrieved July 28, 2021, from https://brands.joinstatus.com/tiktok-influencer-marketing-examples

41. Foxwell, B. (2021, February 18). *TikTok Influencer Marketing: How to Work With Influencers on TikTok*. Iconosquare Blog. https://blog.iconosquare.com/tiktok-influencer-marketing-how-to-work-with-influencers-on-tiktok/

42. R. (2020a, December 14). *How many followers do you need on TikTok to get paid?* Social Public Blog. https://socialpubli.com/blog/how-many-followers-on-tiktok-to-get-paid/

43. Sweigard, K. (2020, June 29). *How to Make Money on TikTok*. Elise Darma. https://elisedarma.com/blog/how-to-make-money-on-tiktok

44. Hayes, R. (2020, December 27). *How To Make Money On TikTok*. Tech Junkie. https://social.techjunkie.com/make-money-tik-tok/#Method_One_Be_An_ldquoInfluencerrdquo

45. Suszka, M. (2021, May 27). *Influencer Monetisation on TikTok: How the Platform is Empowering Creators*. [Talking Influence]. https://talkinginfluence.com/2021/05/25/influe ncer-monetisation-on-tiktok-how-the-platform-is-empowering-creators/

46. V, O. (2021, July 29). *TikTok Monetization for Beginners | How To Start Making Money With The Most Hyped App*. Adsterra Affiliate Marketing and Traffic Monetization Blog. https://adsterra.com/blog/tiktok-monetization-for-beginners/

47. Latimer, J. (2021, May 12). *How to Make Money on TikTok*. Good Financial Cents®. https://www.goodfinancialcents.com/make-money-tiktok/

48. Geyser, W. (2020b, December 30). *12 TikTok Tools to Bolster Your Marketing Efforts*. Influencer Marketing Hub. https://influencermarketinghub.com/tiktok-tools-marketing/

49. Cox, S. (2021a, June 24). *8 Must-Have TikTok Tools to Boost Your Growth*. Filmora.Wondershare. https://filmora.wondershare.com/tiktok/8-must-have-tiktok-tools.html

50. A. (2021a, July 24). *12 Best TikTok Tools on the Market This Year (2021)*. TokUpgrade. https://tokupgrade.com/best-tiktok-tools/#Media_Mister

51. Jones, R. (2021, July 8). *The 12 Best TikTok Tools For Fast Audience Growth in 2021*. Jeffbullas's Blog. https://www.jeffbullas.com/best-tiktok-tools/

52. Grustniy, L. (2020, May 18). *How to protect your TikTok account*. Kaspersky. https://www.kaspersky.com/blog/tiktok-privacy-security/32333/

53. Balaban, D. (2020, August 26). *How to Protect Your TikTok Account from Hackers*. ReadWrite. https://readwrite.com/2020/08/26/how-to-protect-your-tiktok-account-from-hackers/

Made in the USA
Coppell, TX
06 December 2021

67281167R00104